As you   e depth

of a fath.   .... gives you the real truth about hurt and

grief. It is therapeutic even for those who have not experienced the loss

of a child. The roller coaster of emotions and how to deal with them is

expressed with biblical and spiritual revelation. Mark has been honest

with us and tells us how the hurts evoke elements of guilt, anger, and

insufficiency even though we know the solution is found in Him, His

Word, and the guidance of the Holy Spirit. Mark lets us know that

"losing control" is one of our greatest battles that can transport us

to our greatest victory when we acknowledge that He is sovereign.

Mark and Michelle know that God raised their daughter—not like

we had hoped for—but He raised her beyond the human plane to the

everlasting. We miss Aly. We who have a living hope will be reunited,

and grief will cease, pain will be gone, and nothing will separate us

from her ever again.

Dr. Ralph Holland,

President International Missions Network, Founder & President Mundo

de Fe, co-author of *Relentless: Chronicles of Faith, Love and Service.*

Disappointment, unfulfilled dreams and expectations, damaged rela-

tionships, and unexpected tragedies all have one thing in common:

they present a crossroad in our lives. We have to choose the path to

follow. One path leads to further disappointment and one leads to life.

I have known Mark Moore as a colleague, but more importantly as a

close friend. When I was facing my own crossroad, Mark helped me

choose the right path. He did so with integrity and honesty. When

Mark and his family found themselves at their own crossroad, he did the same. This book is raw and honest, which is refreshing. But more than that, it has integrity as its foundation. With that in mind, this book is a setup by God to facilitate deep healing in the hearts of those who have seen their dreams fade. I encourage all who need a fresh perspective on difficult circumstances to read this book and be blessed.

Caleb Camp,
Co-founder, Hope4Nations, author of *The Hospitality of God.*

Very few people can walk through what Mark has walked through and still trust God with their hearts. His book allows you to feel and see what we should all do when faced with adversity. I have always said intelligence quotient is one thing but adversity quotient is the real thing. Mark faced adversity head-on, and when the dust settled, he remained standing. His writings will inspire you to give value to your life and the people in it.

James DeMelo,
Men's Pastor, Covenant Church - Carrollton (Texas), speaker and author of *Andrizo Man: A Call to Distinctive and Authentic Manhood.*

Perception is reality. Well, not necessarily, but for the perceiver, it is. The filter through which we view our world becomes our reality and it creates our destiny. Sadly, sometimes the filter skews the truth and we end up living a lie, or living defeated when God desired victory for us. When life gives us *blue,* we get to choose the shade. We can choose the "blues" or we can take the path of "sky blue yonder" or "deep blue sea." We can't help what happens to us in life, but we get to choose how we react to what happens. Mark and Michelle Moore are daily choosing "sky blue yonder" in the aftermath of the death of their "Aly girl." I pray your heart is as overwhelmingly encouraged as mine has been as you read this book. Mark's words have added new depth to my walk through this life of faith. If your heart is broken today, let the mending begin as you dig into this raw and honest account of tragedy to triumph.

Kevin Herrin,
Pastor, The Fellowship - Texas City (Texas).

It has been my privilege to know Mark and Michelle Moore for many decades and have watched them advance the Kingdom of God faithfully, both here and abroad. Only eternity will fully reveal the harvest to be reaped through their faithful service in the Middle East and among the refugees in that region.

At the time of the tragic accident that took the life of their precious daughter, Alyssa, we united with thousands of intercessors around the world, and watched Mark and Michelle walk through the darkest valley of their lives with courage and strength.

Without hesitation, I highly recommend this book to everyone who has faced personal crises and may need extra strength not only to survive, but thrive in the midst of heartache and disappointment.

May God, our heavenly Father, wrap His arms around every reader and provide peace that passes all human understanding and the strength and courage to fulfill God's calling and purpose in their lives.

Dr. Larry Pyle,
Founder & President Successful Living Concepts, author of *50 Years of Miracles* and *Keeping the Church Relevant.*

Rarely do you come across a book that gives words to something you have felt in your heart and not known how to express. Mark's book does that and more! It is common, the feelings of pain and loss. They are not all the same, and yet we hold them in common. It is equally common, ubiquitous even, to find expressions of those pains and longings, in art, literature, song and movies. What is uncommon is something or someone who truly helps us understand our pain and then begin the long hopeful journey out. Mark's new book will help lead you out of your pain towards healing and wholeness which is found only in Jesus. Thanks Mark.

Jerry Shaffer,
Founding Pastor, The Well – Geneva (Illinois).

The title of the book says it all. Mark Moore has written a book explaining the nightmare of the tragic loss of their beloved daughter and how his wife and he walked through this crisis together and continued their lifelong journey. This book isn't a three-step program on getting over tragedy, but a guide on how God provided them strength through the Bible, prayer, and friends and how we must crawl and then walk through being unrecognizable and shattered. Prepare yourself as you walk hand in hand with the Moore family and experience their lifelong journey in grasping the love of God through this horrific tragedy.

Darryl Carnley,
Founding Pastor, North Pole Worship Center and Co-founder My360project, a worldwide humanitarian organization.

If you've ever experienced loss of any kind in your life, this book is a must-read. In the following pages, Mark courageously and vulnerably bares his soul as he journals their family's journey through the unimaginable loss of their daughter.

As you read their story, you may discover you have not yet processed grief of your own. Perhaps you have lost loved ones during the pandemic, been forced to close a business, give up on a dream, or have lost your career. Perhaps you have suffered tragedy in your life and find yourself needing hope in the middle of the hurt. This book will help you do just that—find light in the darkness and find healing in your pain.

The journey through grief is imperative. We cannot avoid or abandon the process. Attempting to move forward without completing our processes of grieving casts a shadow on every endeavor. Unprocessed grief results in a life lived below its capacity as it is unable to release what was and move forward into the future. This book will help you find a way through your pain and into the future God still has for you.

Jon Ashcraft,
Pastor, CT Church - Pasadena (Texas) and author of *Becoming a Second Mile Leader.*

SHATTERED

FINDING HOPE AND PURPOSE
IN THE MIDST OF DISAPPOINTMENT

MARK A. MOORE

ISBN: 979-8-75914517-2 (Paperback)

First Edition: 2021

Printed in the United States of America

DEDICATION

This book is dedicated to our amazing children, Clarke, Annie, and Carsten. You make life worth living. Also, to our beautiful daughter, Alyssa "Aly" Ruth Moore. Our twenty years with you on this side of eternity can't compare to what you're experiencing now. We miss you every day, Aly Cat. Thank you for the inspiration.

SPECIAL THANKS

My life has been filled with amazing people who have gone before me and paved the way, as well as many who have stood behind me and pushed me to be better. This book and the wisdom found in it are directly influenced by those people. I have had the privilege of standing on the shoulders of giants. I will try to list a few of them and give them the credit they deserve, but I'm sure I will fall way short of what I'm attempting.

The first person and the One who has had the greatest impact on my life is my beautiful and amazing wife, Michelle. She has pushed, prodded, poked, and kicked me to be a better man. She has loved me in spite of it all. It has not been an easy task, but one she has been well-equipped to perform. God knew the perfect partner in life I needed. Thank you, sweetheart, for staying the course. I love you with every ounce of my heart!

To my mom and dad, Jim and Bobbie Moore, words cannot even express how blessed I am to be your son. Out of the billions of possibilities, God chose you to be my parents. There couldn't have been a better choice. You have embodied and exemplified what it looks like to walk this journey of life with joy, passion, and purpose in the midst of storms and disappointments. Thank you for showing me the way.

Pastors Ralph and Donna, thank you for standing with us through years of ministry and never casting stones. You have mentored us and pastored us through the valleys and the mountaintops. We wouldn't be where we are without you. We love you.

Caleb and Lydia, Jay and Mary, you are the very definition of Jesus' words, "Greater love has no one than this, that a person will lay down his life for his friends." You have loved us through it all! Thank you.

Mehmet and Nihal, Jeremey and Michelle, doing ministry with you has truly been an honor and a joy! I have learned so much from each of you. You have redefined the word "team"…it's actually "family."

In Memory of Ricky Texada, pastor and friend. The impact you left on this world cannot be measured this side of eternity. Thank you for leading the way.

CONTENTS

FOREWORD   XIII
PREFACE   XIX
INTRODUCTION   1

1. DISAPPOINTMENT IS NOT THE ENEMY   5
2. GOD IS GOOD   15
3. OUT OF CONTROL   25
4. IT'S MORE THAN I CAN HANDLE   31
5. THE DWELLING PLACE   41
6. CHOICES   51
7. A LOSS OF MOTIVATION   59
8. ALIGNING OUR EXPECTATIONS WITH HIS TRUTH   67
9. WHO SITS ON THE THRONE?   77
10. LIVING IN THE MYSTERY   83
11. LIVING IN THE VALLEY   89
12. THE PLACE OF WORSHIP   95
13. PURSUING HIS PRESENCE   103
14. THE TABLE OF INTIMACY   113
15. THERE IS HOPE IN THE PAIN   117
16. THERE WILL BE SCARS   125
17. BROKENNESS AND VULNERABILITY   131
18. THE PARADOX OF PEACE   137
19. THIS IS NOT OUR HOME   145

FINAL THOUGHTS   149
CONCLUSION   153
NOTES   155

FOREWORD

I have known of Mark and Michelle Moore for more than twenty years. I have always admired their call to ministry in the Middle East with a measure of awe and wonder. Their faithfulness to the Lord and courage to move their family to another part of the world to share the love of Jesus for many years in a predominantly hostile environment is both inspiring and faith provoking. My bride, Amárillys, and I have gotten to know them personally over the last several years and our respect for them has only grown from the interactions. Little did we know that our lives would take our most challenging and crushing turn a mere six months apart from one another.

Our world came to a halt in the form of a living nightmare on the evening of September 23, 2019. Our seventeen-year-old son Gabriel was a private pilot. Amárillys received a call from Gabriel's aviation mentor just after dark that he had disappeared off the tracking system and was believed to have gone down somewhere in a remote part of the mountains on his return trip from Fayetteville, Arkansas. I walked in from running an errand to see the look of concern and hear the tremble in her voice that signals immediately that something bad is happening. After hanging up, our minds began to race. Was he ok? Did he land safely somewhere and just had no ability to communicate? God forbid, could the worst have happened? Our mind and spirit couldn't go there, so we began to fervently pray for his safety and rescue if needed.

September 23 began like any other day. Life was *normal.* Gabriel had worked the first day of a new job he was really excited about and was killing it studying for his instrument rating certification as a pilot. He had his first solo flight at the age of sixteen and had successfully earned his private pilot's license at seventeen. Just a few months shy of his eighteenth birthday, he was on track to realize his dream of becoming a commercial pilot. He was highly motivated, strong-willed, and didn't allow any obstacle to hold him back from attacking his goals and defeating challenges. Around four o'clock in the afternoon, he reminded me he was taking a friend home to get back to the University of Arkansas after attending a funeral in our hometown of McKinney, Texas, over the weekend. Gabriel needed the flight hours, and his friend would get back much quicker and avoid missing classes. He yelled, "See you later, Dad," and he rushed out the garage door to get to the airport. His voice still echoes in my mind with the crushing reality that those were the last words I would ever hear him speak to me again on this side of eternity. "See you bud, be careful," I yelled back.

After about an hour or so, I had my first of a few very frustrating phone calls with the local county sheriff's dept. that had been dispatched for search and rescue. Cell phone coverage was nonexistent where Gabriel had disappeared, and where witnesses had heard a plane in trouble was not easy to get to. They had no information to give us even though slight bits of information were already being leaked by local news stations.

We prayed HARDER. We contacted some of our fiercest prayer warriors and asked them to join in for his safe return. We worshipped! We declared Scriptures about divine protection, Gabriel's destiny...we threw the spiritual warfare kitchen sink at the situation. We had hope and faith he was somehow fine. The night dragged on.

Hours went by without any definitive word from the sheriff on his whereabouts or condition. Yet, once again, a local news station updated their story that there was a small plane that had crashed in the general vicinity of Prairie Grove, Arkansas. Where was the Lord in all of this? We were hurt, angry, frightened, and still holding on to the belief in the goodness of God that it would still turn out okay. Shortly after another very frustrating call with the sheriff's office there was a knock on our door. It was about 1:30 in the morning, and I opened the door to two fully uniformed McKinney police officers. This was it. My heart sank, more like plummeted to an emotional place I had never experienced. But it turned out the officers only knew there was a crash and had no new information. Their visit only brought more confusion and frustration.

I sat back down on the couch and began to scroll news networks once again. Still praying, still worshipping, still declaring God's Scriptures that we were so certain before would protect us and our family against a tragedy like this. After all, we had served the Lord in full-time ministry for over nineteen years. We were his favored kids and doing everything we knew to be faithful to Jesus and to our calling. Surely there was a miracle about to take place, right?

Then I saw it. An NBC affiliate in Fayetteville was reporting a single-person fatality in a plane crash near Prairie Grove. I was sitting just a few inches away from Amárillys. I froze in shock. I can tell you now from experience, the only thing that equals the gut-wrenching news that your teenage son has tragically died is sitting in silence for several minutes trying to figure out how to tell the mother that birthed him that he was gone. Then the task had to be excruciatingly repeated a few hours later with Gabriel's then fifteen-year old brother, Joel, and ten-year old brother, Liam. This wasn't supposed to be our story!

Gabriel's personality and drive was a force of nature. He was assured to fulfill an amazing destiny. He was supposed to bring glory to the Lord by living out a long, impactful, and faithful life. However, this was part of our story now. And we would begin a new painful journey without Gabriel whether we liked it or not.

It has been two years and almost two months since that fateful day as I write this foreword. We have learned more about the grieving process and what it means to believe God is good no matter the circumstance than we signed up for. Or is that true? Perhaps we did sign up for this when we dedicated our lives to the Lord, as well as our children, when they were born.

The truth is the Scriptures and the words of the Lord Himself make it quite clear. In this world we *will* have *tribulation.* Our promise from the Lord stops short of a guarantee we will not suffer in this broken world; in fact, it is assured we will. It won't look or perhaps even feel the same for everyone, but eventually everyone will face tribulation. If you are not familiar with this word, it is the Greek word thlip'-sis: pressure (literally or figuratively):- afflicted, anguish, burdened, persecution trouble. The *Encyclopedia of Biblical Words* defines it this way: the idea of great emotional or spiritual stress that can be caused by external or internal pressure.

It becomes a stark reality and no one knows what it feels like more than Jesus. Read about His very personal experience in the Garden of Gethsemane prior to suffering the beating and hanging on the cross he endured, passionately, for you and me. Case closed. This is also why we can be assured the Lord knows exactly how to carry us through our pain and times of extreme disappointment.

For the record, time does NOT heal the pain. Time may diminish the emotional effects of pain, but a scar of pain remains. I wouldn't have it any other way. The pain is great because of the great love and relationship shared. What I have learned in this journey is that Jesus is greater than my pain. He is greater than we think. His ability to love us, touch us, heal us, comfort us, guide us and lead us knows no bounds. Perhaps the most telling evidence of this is that he does not demand that we stay in lock-step with Him along the way. He is not offended by our anger, confusion, questions, emotional process, warped thinking—any of our flawed human traits. He simply LOVES us through it all.

As I stated in the beginning, little did Mark, Michelle, Amárillys and I, let alone our kids, have any idea how our lives would be turned upside down in such hauntingly familiar ways. We are both now part of a community we didn't want to belong to.

In this book Mark shares so many of the poignant truths of what it is like to suffer great loss in the face of faith, hope, and the promises of God. As I said before, I have admired the Moore family's fearlessness in the face of great opposition in their unique calling to the Middle East. Mark's strength and courage in writing this book may be his most awe-inspiring feat yet. Their story is complicated, messy, and perhaps the most real thing that will ever truly test of how you see and interact with our heavenly Father.

I believe Mark very accurately portrays the strange space you find yourself in when you can simultaneously experience pain and peace, despair and hope, grief and joy. I don't believe there's a formula for grieving or moving on with life amid great loss or disappointment, but I do believe there are common patterns. I have come to believe walking through impossibly painful times requires an honesty in our relationship with God that nothing else would ever produce. Mark so delicately and succinctly lets us into his own journey through his process…the good, the bad, the ugly, and the beautiful reality of the Gospel in the thick of the human condition.

I have no doubt if you have ever suffered, which I am sure you have, that you will gain insight, strength, and perhaps most important, hope as you read. There is a greater purpose for our lives than we often recognize, certainly a greater purpose for our pain than to get stuck in one life-defining moment.

This book is chock full of the challenging intersection between truth in the word of God and the fragility of the human experience. Mark's personal journey and raw thoughts lead us right back to the place where we need to end up—in the presence of Jesus. *We may be shattered, but we're **never** abandoned.*

Clint Hatton,
Pastor, Gates Church – McKinney (Texas),
Founder of BigBoldBrave.

PREFACE

When I stop to think what so many of us have lost or fought through in 2020, it can be overwhelming. This past year has brought struggles, pain, and disappointment. It has been difficult as we've battled with disease, separation, depression, loss, and fear of the unknown. Rarely has our world been more divided or our future more uncertain. Yet, it's quite possible many reading this book have struggled for years with unmet expectations, unexpected loss, and the pain associated with them. The truth of the matter is no one and no season is exempt. Life brings struggle and disappointment to everyone and every season of life.

For our family, this season of our lives has been a fog. In many respects it's been like a bad dream from which you keep hoping to wake up. I've hesitated to share too many of my thoughts during our journey as I don't want to pull others into the deluge of pain and disappointment we've experienced as we've walked through the loss of our daughter and the many other changes in our lives that came in 2020.

However, we've received many notes and messages from people who have been encouraged by our journey. Because of that, I have decided to share our story as it unfolds. Not all of my thoughts and conclusions will be accurate as they're still raw and incomplete. Many things may get edited later and corrected; some might just go uncorrected because I don't have any other answers. We're still seeking and learning to be okay with those things that may remain mysteries this side of eternity.

I've cried a lot while writing this book. It's been both painful and healing. I believe both are necessary to bring us through the valley. I hope, as you read the words on these pages, you will allow yourself to experience pain and healing as well. And in this process, may you also find the fire that burns so hot for you in Jesus Christ.

Some may choose to walk past this book because they feel they've never experienced the level of grief that would warrant reading it. If that's you, please reconsider. This book is not solely written for those who have lost a loved one, but attempts to pull back the curtain on disappointments and the losses that result from them, at every level.

My prayer is this book will challenge your perceptions about disappointment and radically change your relationship with our heavenly Father. Whether you've walked through the depths of darkness and grief or you've just been "rattled" by life's constant disappointments, there is something for you within these pages. A new perspective and a fresh walk with God awaits.

INTRODUCTION

"In the beginning was the Word, and the Word was with God,
and the Word was God. He was in the beginning with God.
All things were made through him, and without him was not
any thing made that was made.
In him was life, and the life was the light of men.
The light shines in the darkness,
and the darkness has not overcome it."

John 1:1-5 (ESV)

I never thought this would be my life. Instead, I thought this is what "other" people went through. Our family had sacrificed too much for God to allow something like this to be our new normal. It didn't line up with how I expected God would protect me and my family.

We gave everything for the Kingdom of God, so for some crazy reason, I thought we were different, protected. Our marriage would be amazing. Sure, not perfect, but blessed and much better than average. Our children would grow up serving the Lord and never have the issues my wife, Michelle, and I had to deal with. They would also marry people who served the Lord, and they would have amazing children whom Michelle and I would spoil rotten (as all good grandparents do).

You can imagine my surprise when our marriage struggled while we served the Lord on the mission field. Maybe "struggled" is an understatement. We had problems. Big ones. Then, our children began to have problems, following a course Michelle and I were all too familiar with.

Of course when you live thousands of miles away, it's easy to hide and not be honest and open about what you're going through. We swept many of the problems we had "under the rug," buried and hidden. Yet, my attitude didn't change..."Look what we're doing for the Lord! Certainly He will fix us."

Chalk it up to naiveté or self-delusion, but I believed the world didn't rotate the same way around the Moore family. We were supposed to be special. We had already sacrificed so much.

I realize my transparent or straightforward explanation may come across as arrogant, but it was more ignorance and wishful thinking than anything else. I was afraid of losing what I had. So, I created a set of expectations where everything I loved was supernaturally protected.

We all have expectations for how our lives will turn out and what our journeys will look like. Maybe the expectations only exist in our minds and are never actually expressed, but we have them all the same. These are our hopes and dreams, and sometimes our fears. But, they are also our disappointments when our story doesn't follow the plot we had written.

Disappointments are the result of expectations, expressed or unexpressed, realized or unrealized, that have not been met. When an expectation is not met, it becomes a loss. Many times that loss results in unexpected changes and directions in life. Maybe it was the loss of a career or marriage. Maybe it was a broken relationship or a child born with deformities.

The reality is each of us will have many disappointments in life. When we are in the middle of them, they all seem like more than we can handle, and many times they actually are.

Michelle and I have walked through disappointments. We've seen dreams that didn't pan out (at least not in the way or in the timing we had expected), broken relationships we thought would be "forever" friendships, a miscarriage, and most recently, the tragic and sudden loss of our twenty-year old daughter. So yeah, we understand disappointment and grief.

Suddenly we find ourselves thrown into the harsh realities of life, stretched out on the rocks; battered, beaten, broken, and bruised. The ink on the pages of our story is smudged and barely recognizable. This is NOT how we planned our life together. It doesn't look anything like we thought it should.

Michelle's and my faith has taken a beating. Yet, it's emerging stronger and with greater understanding than ever before. We are discovering, through experience, our faith isn't meant to be born out of ignorance, fear, or what we see. Rather, its foundation is laid by how we worship when our outcomes don't match up to our expectations.

Ultimately, through sharing our journey and by being as vulnerable and transparent as possible, I hope our struggles, failures, and victories might be a light of hope for others—especially for those walking through disappointment, discouragement and grief.

Maybe you're going through a season of life similar to this or you've just made it to the other side of such a journey. It's important to know, even when things seem their darkest, God is good.

DISAPPOINTMENT IS NOT THE ENEMY

*"There can be no deep disappointment
where there is not deep love."*

~ Dr. Martin Luther King, Jr.
(Baptist minister and civil rights leader)

Our story of disappointment and grief began on our way to church. I was set to preach that Sunday, and Michelle decided, while we were driving, to call our daughter who lived 6,000 miles away in Dallas, Texas. Of course it was 1:30 in the morning there (we lived and pastored in the modern-day city of Ephesus in Turkey), but Aly had said she would be awake late since it was the Fourth of July.

Our hearts sank into our feet when a man from the Deputy Sheriff's office answered Aly's phone. He informed us she had been care-flighted to a hospital and was in critical condition after an accident on an all-terrain vehicle (ATV). A few hours later, while Michelle rushed to America, our daughter went on to be with her Heavenly Father.

Our lives took a sudden turn and put us on a road we never expected to be on. Our future was planned, we knew where we were headed. Now everything was uncertain, and we were lost with no idea where we would end up.

AVOIDING THE PAIN

One of the biggest obstacles to God's plans and purposes for our lives comes when we mishandle sudden changes in direction. Even good changes can feel uncomfortable when our expectations are to continue going straight ahead toward our goals. Consequently, we feel lost, confused, and disoriented by unmet expectations and the disappointments resulting from them.

I say this because there are right ways and wrong ways to handle the process of change that comes from our seasons of pain. How we deal with them will ultimately put us on a path forward into new and exciting territory or on a path that leads us backward or sideways looking for where things went wrong.

When we experience pain, our first response tends to be to find a way to make it stop. A few weeks after our daughter passed, probably because of the stress and grief, my back went out. I've had back pain off and on my entire adult life, but this episode sent me to the emergency care clinic. I was in so much pain I couldn't even wiggle my toes without crying out. Not once in the middle of the pain did I stop to ask, "How did this happen?" The only thing I could think of was, "What do I need to do to make it stop?" I wasn't looking for a path through the pain. I simply wanted relief.

It's difficult enough when the pain is physical, but when that pain comes from disappointment and unmet expectations, it can be even worse. Also, the results of trying to avoid or eliminate the pain can be more far-reaching. In our attempts to stop the hurting and find solutions for our situation, we can lose our direction and our passion for life...or worse, we lose our faith.

One reason we tend to lose our way in times of disappointment is we have the expectation it will never happen to us.

So let's be real. It's not a matter of "if" you'll walk through disappointments, but "when."

"Consider it nothing but joy, my brothers and sisters,
whenever *you fall into various trials."* James 1:2 (AMP)

In this passage, James, the leader of the church in Jerusalem and the brother of Jesus, states a simple fact, "whenever." Not if, not maybe, but WHEN. He is trying to properly set our expectations.

No one likes trials, especially the costly ones. Trials and sufferings are often born out of disappointment or they are the soil from which disappointment is formed. Disappointment brings about grief and pain. So, we run from it and try to hide when it comes close to catching us.

In Michelle's and my journey through grief, we've discovered at its core we will find disappointment. We grieve because we're disappointed. I'm disappointed I won't see Aly on this side of eternity again; I'm disappointed because I will never walk her down the aisle, hold my grandchildren, and watch my daughter become the woman of God I had always hoped and believed she would be. But, our daughter is with Jesus, so why should we grieve?

Instead, what do we do? Well, there were days I just wanted to hide, sit in the corner, throw a blanket over my pain, and be very still and silent. I wanted to make the pain go away and ignore the pounding on the door, the fear, the anger, and the unbelief.

I remember one day in particular, a few weeks after our daughter passed away, we had people at our house. Everyone began to reminisce about Aly. I wasn't ready for those conversations and realized I was about to lose it.

The reality of what we had lost fell on me in that moment. So, I went to the only place I could hide, our closet. I laid on the floor and cried for thirty minutes until Michelle came and found me. I'm not talking the crying you do when you hit your knee on the bottom of the kitchen table. I'm talking about the screaming into the pillow, red-faced, snot-dripping-on-the-floor kind of crying. I just wanted it to stop. I wanted my daughter back. I wanted the nightmare to be over and for my sleeping self to wake up.

The pain was more than I could handle.

I wanted the Lord to return and not to have to go on with this life; not to have to "press in and press on" without my little girl. I was angry with the Lord for not "protecting" my daughter and fulfilling what I believed was His promise to make my life wonderful.

So here I was. Everything was wrong and nothing made sense. This was not supposed to be my life. It was unrecognizable.

At some point in our disappointment, we'll be faced with a dilemma. Do we avoid it, or do we dive in with both feet and deal with it head on? Will the disappointments of life take us out or will we allow them to take us deep?

The reality is everyone is different in how they approach pain, grief and disappointment. Michelle has approached this process very differently from me. For me, pictures, clothing, anything that reminded me of Aly or had belonged to Aly became painful, and most days still is. For Michelle, she pulled all those things close. I wanted, at all costs, to avoid the reminders of my precious girl. To me, it seemed Michelle wanted to swim in them.

No approach is perfect or necessarily the "right" one. However, of the two extremes, Michelle may have had the better one. In retrospect, I feel my approach placed disappointment and grief square in the camp of the enemy. Losing a child was my greatest fear in life, and here I was walking through the pain and sorrow that goes with it. It felt unbearable. Instead of embracing the pain and accepting the grace that God sends with it, I allowed it to become something I should either avoid or attack.

What I'm discovering is disappointment and grief were not designed to be the enemy; it's just our fear of pain puts them there.

THE DEPTHS OF DISAPPOINTMENT

Before our daughter passed away, I had never experienced a loss that brought this much pain. I thought I had a decent understanding of grief. After all, I am a pastor and should know these things, right? Yet, I've actually been surprised by the depth of it. Just when I think I've gone as deep as I could, I discover another layer of pain, more gut-wrenching than before.

Not to be cliché, but it truly is like an onion; you pull another layer off, thinking you're coming to the end, only to find many more layers—each one going deeper and becoming stronger, more pungent. Before long, your eyes are burning and tearing up, and you can barely see the way out.

Several months later as I write this, I realize I don't cry as often as I used to. However, when I do, it's just as deep and painful as that first day when I realized my baby girl was gone. My choices can be to forget Aly and avoid the pain, hoping it will go away; or carry her with me, remembering who she was and allowing that pain to transform me, make me better, and lead me down a new path with a different, but amazing end from what I imagined. However, in order to do that, I must also carry the pain and disappointment of the loss.

Layers. So many layers.

Here's the thing—God can use disappointment and grief in our lives to bring us to a place where we relinquish our constant struggle to take control of our surroundings. It's often in that place of brokenness where God and His strength become our sole focus.

It's in those moments when, hopefully, we begin to realize that disappointment and grief don't have to be the enemy. I'm finding that love has no weight without grief. Grief IS "weighty." If you allow it, it can pull you down to depths that have no light. You can get lost in the dark places, where the ***true enemy***, the deceiver, the destroyer, finds his grip.

There have been days when Michelle and I have stayed home, hurt and crying. There have also been days when we've celebrated, laughed, and remembered. Healing can emerge in the deep places as long as we keep our anchor in Christ. We're learning to buoy our grief in His abundant and tangible grace, so we can explore the depths and still be *in the light.* God's abounding grace is how love finds its grip on grief and rises. In other words, it's God's grace and compassion that leads us through the dark confines of our pain.

When grief slams into us like the tide does the coast on a stormy night, we should not be so surprised. Scripture says we will walk through stormy, turbulent seasons. It's life. We live in ALL the seasons. So why does it continue to catch us off guard when spring and summer end and the storms of fall and winter come? If we are truly followers of Jesus Christ, then we've got a sea wall to protect us, a strong tower.

> *"The name of the LORD is a strong tower; the righteous run to it and are safe."* Proverbs 18:10 (NKJV)

The issue is we tend to run from our trials, trying to avoid the storms of life, rather than running to our strong tower in the midst of the storms, giving Him our grief and allowing Him to protect us while the storms rage. It doesn't mean we won't experience pain and suffering, rather, in the midst of our pain and our suffering, we have a Savior. In the midst of all the wind, rain, thunder, and lightning, we can find joy and peace and be transformed into the image of the One who calms the storms.

The Apostle Paul explains it like this:

> *"And not only this, but [with joy] let us exult in our sufferings and rejoice in our hardships, knowing that hardship (distress, pressure, trouble) produces patient endurance;*

*and endurance, proven character (spiritual maturity); and
proven character, hope and confident assurance [of eternal
salvation]. Such hope [in God's promises] never disappoints
us, because God's love has been abundantly poured out within
our hearts through the Holy Spirit who was given to us."*
(Romans 5:3-5 AMP)

Notice what it *doesn't* say. It does not say, "Let us run away
from our sufferings or ignore our hardships...." Rather, Paul
says, *"WITH JOY* let us *EXULT* in our sufferings and *REJOICE*
in our hardships...."

Paul, you have got to be kidding me!

Obviously, he never had to suffer or he would not have been so
cavalier about it. We laugh at that, because we know in reality, Paul
understood suffering better than anyone. He modeled it for the rest
of us. That's why he could write about it and make the claims he
made. He found a way through the storm, and he had plenty of
them to walk through.

GOD USES EVERYTHING

When we begin to fully understand God is truly for us and NOT
against us, we can believe He will use our worst moments to make
them our greatest victories.

A.W. Tozer in his book *The Crucified Life* wrote, "If we
understand that everything happening to us is to make us more
Christlike, it will solve a great deal of anxiety in our lives."[1]

EVERYTHING. He uses everything to make us more like Him!
He is for you, He is not against you! He will take your victories,
successes, failures, pain, your broken heart, and your disappointments, and He will use them to create something stunningly
beautiful. And why wouldn't He?

"What then shall we say to these things? If God is for us, who can be against us? He who did not spare his own Son but gave him up for us all, how will he not also with him graciously give us all things?" (Romans 8:31-32 ESV)

We've got to get this in us…God went to the deepest depths possible to make certain that we could be in fellowship with Him. This understanding needs to be the very air we breathe. When God's ultimate sacrifice of His Son for our victory becomes our focus, the disappointments of life become a strong foundation (as opposed to a weight around our necks) our Heavenly Father can build His house upon.

Did you know?

Disappointment is a result of loving deeply. Consequently, when we experience a broken relationship or a loss, we'll be faced with the option of running and hiding or allowing the pain to draw us closer to the Lord. Disappointment is not the enemy, but a tool the Lord will use to make us into His image.

"Our best successes often come after
our greatest disappointments."

~ Henry Ward Beecher

(19th century clergyman, social reformer, and speaker)

Prayer

Dear Heavenly Father,

When I think of the suffering and pain your Son endured on my behalf, I am reminded of the pain you must have carried during that time. You didn't run from it, you didn't send your angels to remove your only begotten Son from the cross. Instead, you walked through it because you loved me so much. Give me strength to walk through my current situation. Help me to endure the pain, knowing you are faithful and you are with me. Make me better through this journey and draw me closer to you. Use everything. I surrender to your plan and your will for my life. I love you.

In your Son's precious name, Amen.

GOD IS GOOD

*"Faith is a free surrender and a joyous wager
on the unseen, unknown, untested goodness of God."*

~ Martin Luther

(Central figure in the Protestant Reformation)

Whether disappointment is allowed to do its work in us or not comes down to this question: Is God good?

After Michelle's flight arrived in the United States, our pastor met her at the airport, and they went straight to the hospital. I joined her twenty-four hours later with our two youngest kids. Our oldest son, Clarke, had flown in from Redding, California.

They kept Aly on life support because we had agreed to make her an organ donor. That gave us three days to pray for a miracle. The doctors had informed us she had no blood flow to her brain, but we believed there was still room for God to show up and do what only He could do. For three days we sat by her side and prayed with every ounce of faith we had, and so did thousands upon thousands around the world.

Those three days are forever etched in our hearts and minds as they were our last days to hold our daughter and love her into eternity.

Michelle and I have always believed in the power of the Holy Spirit. We believe the same God who healed during the days of Jesus and the Apostles heals today—the same power that raised Jesus from the dead is active and alive today, healing and restoring lives. In fact, His command in Matthew 10 was, *"...go, preach, saying, 'The kingdom of heaven is at hand.' Heal the sick, cleanse the lepers, raise the dead, cast out demons. Freely you have received, freely give."* (NKJV)

THE CONFLICT OF LOSS

The conflict for us has been reconciling the loss of our daughter, when so many people from around the world prayed for her restoration. If I'm honest, and I'm trying to be, we've wrestled with our faith. Why didn't He heal our daughter? Why didn't He raise her from the dead? Why didn't we get our miracle?

We may never have the complete answers to all our questions. But, here's what we do know—since Aly's accident, and because of the testimony of the way she lived her life, many have come into the kingdom. Many who had fallen away from the Lord have recommitted their lives to Him and to His kingdom, and many who walked with the Lord have realized they need a reviving, a reawakening of their purpose. I also know this—we prayed for her healing, and she is healed in a way we all long for.

The bottom line is, we didn't get "our" miracle, but Aly got hers.

I'm beginning to look differently at the miraculous, signs, wonders, and the supernatural. Michelle and I have experienced firsthand the healing power of God at work in the world today. We've prayed for people and have watched as the Lord healed them, and we've seen physical and emotional healing in our lives personally.

In fact, Aly's journey with God began this way. She had been in dance classes since she was young. Several years ago, however, she began having knee problems and had to wear a brace during classes. In 2018, while we were at Bethel Church in Redding, California, we went to their Healing Rooms. Aly was brought to the front, and they began to pray for her knee. She was seventeen years old and skeptical. She didn't want to be there. The team began to pray for her, and you could see the shock begin to form on her face; her eyes went wide open, and she began to cry. Afterwards, she told us she could literally feel the knee healing as they prayed. She never had another problem with her knees after that.

As a result, she was forever changed. On that day, she encountered the love of God in a way that could never be expressed with words. The thing is, God was not after her physical healing, He was after her heart. Consequently, she made the decision to attend Bethel's School of Supernatural Ministry (BSSM) the following school year. She finished eighteen months of high school in nine months and was accepted to BSSM the following year. God did in five minutes what Michelle and I had been trying to do for seventeen years. He captured her heart, and she was never the same.

As amazing as this experience was for our family, we have to be careful not to put God in a box of our experiences and establish our theology around that box. For me, in the past, it wasn't a miracle if it didn't play out exactly the way I thought it should; if it didn't fit into my limited, finite understanding of what I felt should happen in each situation.

The reality is I am not God. I do not see the beginning from the end. And, this is also true—God is good. All the time. In every situation. He IS the miraculous. He IS the supernatural. We prayed for a miracle. We prayed for signs and wonders. We prayed for Aly's healing and resurrection. My expected miracle was that she would live, be resurrected and whole.

We received exactly what we prayed for, just not in the package we wanted.

So we have to ask ourselves, do we abandon our faith because God did not do what we expected Him to do? Do we abandon our faith because our disappointment in the outcome means God is not who we believed Him to be?

Pastor and Christian Apologist, Timothy Keller says, "If you say: I believed in God, I trusted God and He didn't come through - You only trusted God to meet your agenda."[2]

When things go wrong and disappointment seems to rule the day, we have to separate our circumstances from His goodness. There will be times and situations where it's okay to say "God is good, but this is not."

Expectations and faith can go hand in hand or they can run counter to each other. It all depends on where our expectations are placed. Are they placed in the outcome or are they placed in who He is?

You see, if our expectations are anchored in the outcome, we will be disappointed and lose faith when the outcome does not match up with what we expected. God's goodness will come into question, and we will be in danger of losing faith in Him.

In Scripture, James tells us *everything* good is from the Father. In Him there is nothing evil. However, we can be tempted and deceived by the enemy. Our expectations can be misdirected and lured away from God's plan and agenda. That is why it is so important to recognize the seasons we are in, that we have an enemy and that God is not him. God is good all the time, and that never changes, but our circumstances do.

> *"Blessed is the man who remains steadfast under trial, for when he has stood the test he will receive the crown of life, which God has promised to those who love him. Let no one say when he is tempted, "I am being tempted by God," for God cannot be tempted with evil, and he himself tempts no one. But each person is tempted when he is lured and enticed by his own desire. Then desire when it has conceived gives birth to sin, and sin when it is fully grown brings forth death.*

*Do not be deceived, my beloved brothers. Every good gift
and every perfect gift is from above, coming down from the
Father of lights, with whom there is no variation or shadow
due to change."* (James 1:17 ESV)

So, if our expectations are anchored in who we know God to
be, and He never changes, then regardless of the outcome we can
take comfort in the knowledge God is good and every good thing
comes from Him. Always. In every circumstance.

So, if the outcome doesn't line up with what we hoped for or
expected, we know that ultimately, the outcome will be good—even
if it's not what we wanted, even if it doesn't mesh with our plans
or agenda, because He is good.

Bill Johnson, pastor and author of *God is Good: He's Better
Than You Think,* says, "We don't have the capacity to exaggerate
God's goodness. We can distort it, or even misrepresent it, but we
can never exaggerate it."[3]

Regardless of our emotions, we must incorporate that statement
into our belief system. It must become our worldview, our overriding
perspective on everything we encounter and struggle through. It's
the only way we can keep from misrepresenting and underestimat-
ing His goodness.

KEEPING OUR FAITH

Pastor and best-selling author, Myles Monroe, said, "Your faith is
only as strong as the crisis it survives."[4] This is a foundational truth.
The size of the crisis will always uncover the depths of your faith.

In the middle of a crisis, disappointment, or personal failure, we
keep our faith by knowing who He is and His plans and purposes
for us are good, better than we think. When we do this in the midst
of our pain and hold on to our faith, then, when prayers seem to go
unanswered (as in our story with Aly), we do not stay discouraged.

Instead, we move into another level of faith, understanding, and commitment, knowing His purpose will be fulfilled. We pray with increased passion and fervor, and we do not let the enemy win through disappointment, discouragement, and despair.

One of my all-time favorite passages (I say that about a lot of verses. because they're all so very good!) is 2 Corinthians 4: 6-12 ESV:

> *"⁶ For God, who said, 'Let light shine out of darkness,' has shone in our hearts to give the light of the knowledge of the glory of God in the face of Jesus Christ. ⁷ But we have this treasure in jars of clay, to show that the surpassing power belongs to God and not to us. ⁸ We are afflicted in every way, but not crushed; perplexed, but not driven to despair; ⁹ persecuted, but not forsaken; struck down, but not destroyed; ¹⁰ always carrying in the body the death of Jesus, so that the life of Jesus may also be manifested in our bodies. ¹¹ For we who live are always being given over to death for Jesus' sake, so that the life of Jesus also may be manifested in our mortal flesh. ¹² So death is at work in us, but life in you."*

God's goodness is not based on our circumstances. His goodness is based on the fact that while death may be at work in us and our situations, the resurrection life of Jesus Christ is actually IN US! So even in our affliction and pain, we are not crushed. Though we may be confused or perplexed, we are not driven to discouragement or despair. When we feel lost, attacked, or struck down, we are not forgotten, forsaken, or destroyed.

His goodness is best seen and understood when His light shines out of our darkness.

After reading this, you may come to the conclusion that Michelle and I have found victory over these areas in our lives. That would not be entirely true. While we are learning to walk victoriously through our grief, we still struggle and we still fail.

As I'm writing this, we are still dealing with the disappointment and grief of losing our daughter. We still struggle in our marriage and with our children. We still have dark days and weeks, and we have days where the darkness seems to win. That's because it's not always easy getting what is in your head to move into your heart, especially when the disappointment is so deep and painful. It takes time, and these measures are not overnight fixes. It requires a willingness to fail and the consistency and determination to get up and try again.

The key to everything is not to quit, but to stay the course. Because of our experience, because we've been knocked down and have continued to get back up, we know that, eventually, we will walk in the victory already purchased for us. God is good and He is for us, not against us. He has proven Himself faithful time and time again.

However, this type of tenacity is not discovered the first time you fall down or are discouraged, and it's not lost the first time you fail to immediately get back up. It's after you get up repeatedly that an attitude of determination finds its footing in your life.

This is why failure and disappointment are a significant and essential part of our growth. It's on these things that God begins to build strength and character. It's the "iron sharpening iron" principal. Its purpose is to make us "sharper." However sometimes the sparks create fires that seem to burn our hopes to the ground.

"For this very reason, make every effort to supplement your faith with virtue, and virtue with knowledge, ⁶and knowledge with self-control, and self-control with steadfastness, and steadfastness with godliness, ⁷and godliness with brotherly affection, and brotherly affection with love. ⁸For if these qualities are yours and are increasing, they keep you

from being ineffective or unfruitful in the knowledge of our Lord Jesus Christ. [9]For whoever lacks these qualities is so nearsighted that he is blind, having forgotten that he was cleansed from his former sins. [10]Therefore, brothers, be all the more diligent to confirm your calling and election, for if you practice these qualities you will never fall."
(2 Peter 1:5-10 ESV)

It's in these seemingly "hopeless" moments, in our darkest trials, that we discover who we are. Greatness in our lives is almost always built on top of struggle, difficulties, failures, and disappointments. It's why we are called "followers" of Christ, and His path journeyed through the cross. However, it didn't end there. When we follow Jesus, there will be suffering, pain, and struggle, but the path will always end in victory, because He is for us and not against us. He is GOOD!

Did you know?

The enemy uses loss and disappointment to try and change our understanding of God's goodness. Once we begin to lessen God's goodness, everything else we believe about our Heavenly Father and His Word is called into question. God is good. All the time. When we truly believe that, we can withstand any disappointment because we know He will turn it to our best benefit.

"This is true faith, a living confidence in the goodness of God."
~ Martin Luther

Prayer

Dear Heavenly Father,

My faith right now is weak. My circumstances seem to be winning, and I need a fresh perspective from your Holy Spirit. I release my limited understanding, and I recognize my responses have been influenced by my situation. You are good all the time and in every circumstance. I lay my understanding, emotions, pain, and disappointment at your feet. I trust you. I love you.

In Jesus' name, Amen.

OUT OF CONTROL

"Never be afraid to trust an unknown future to a known God."

~ Corrie Ten Boom

(Author and Dutch Christian Holocaust survivor)

LOSING CONTROL

Knowing the goodness of God is a central theme when discussing the issues of faith. If we are not confident in His goodness, our faith will fail every time. When our faith in God fails, then the only one left to trust is ourselves. We try to take control of the pain, emotions, and circumstances and steer them in a direction that's favorable and usually less painful.

In the days following Aly's death, I had so many questions. The number one question that ran through my mind was, "What could I have done to prevent this?" I started saying things like, "I should have never let her leave our house. I should have kept her close." There were many days I would literally shake my head trying to wake up from the dream. I just knew it had to be a dream. I still have days like that. "This can't possibly be real, so how can I fix it?"

There have been many times in my life when I've felt like I had lost control of a situation or circumstance, but I always had a sense I could get it back with some hard work and just a little ingenuity (short for manipulation). This time though, I was completely off the rails, and nothing I could do would get us back on track. For possibly the first time in my life, I felt completely lost and out of control.

One of the most difficult revelations I have had to come to terms with on this journey is I never really had any control over anything. My belief that I was in control of my life, family, and ministry was just a myth, a puff of air I constantly tried to hold in my hand. I wasn't able to be there to protect my daughter and there was NOTHING I could have done about it. I wasn't in control.

"I am the vine; you are the branches. Whoever abides in me and I in him, he it is that bears much fruit, for apart from me you can do nothing." (John 15:5 ESV)

Nothing.

That was a difficult conclusion to come to because I have three other children and a wife. The glass house I had built representing my world, shattered on the day Aly died, and I realized something could happen to my other children as well, and there would be little, if anything, I could do to stop it. I couldn't put them in a box and set them on a "safe" shelf where nothing could hurt them.

So, I quietly panicked every time they would leave the house without me. I fought back fear when our oldest son returned to California after Aly's funeral. I struggled with panic attacks when I thought about our two youngest growing up and moving away. I quietly cried the first time my wife returned to the Middle East for two weeks without me (even though it was my idea). I felt helpless and lost in this new world I found myself in, a world I couldn't predict or control.

Speaker and best-selling Christian author, Lysa TerKeurst, in her book *It's Not Supposed to Be This Way: Finding Unexpected Strength When Disappointments Leave You Shattered*, wrote:

"Humans are very attached to outcomes. We say we trust God but behind the scenes we work our fingers to the bone and our emotions into a tangled fray trying to control our outcomes. We praise God when our normal looks like what we thought it would. We question God when it doesn't. And walk away from Him when we have a sinking suspicion that God is the one who set fire to the hope that was holding us together." [5]

GOD WANTS CONTROL

Here's the thing. God doesn't set fire to our hopes and dreams, even though we may suspect Him of doing it. But God will use those fires in our lives to bring us to a place where we relinquish our constant struggle to take control of our surroundings.

God wants our *total* reliance on Him, but He also wants us to relinquish control willingly. That being said, He's not opposed to using our disappointments and pain to begin prying control from our fingers.

That's because He's a good Father. For us to be everything He has ordained us to be, we MUST learn this lesson: only He can steer the ship. Anything else is not His best and will not give us the results we desire.

The Apostle Paul wrote these words to the church in Ephesus,

"Through our union with Christ we too have been claimed by God as his own inheritance. Before we were even born, he gave us our destiny; that we would fulfill the plan of God who always accomplishes every purpose and plan in his heart."
(Ephesians 1:11 TPT)

Solomon writes it this way,

*"Within your heart you can make plans for your future, but
the Lord chooses the steps you take to get there."*
(Proverbs 16:9 TPT)

In other words we are in this *together* with our Heavenly Father.
He loves our plans and our passion to do His work on Earth. He
encourages our dreams and our visions, but He wants to lead us on
that journey. He is the captain of our ship, the creator and purveyor
of our purpose and destiny. Only He can see the end from the
beginning and, consequently, should be the only one at the helm.

If He doesn't have that place in your heart, if you still maintain
a measure of control over the direction of your emotions, beliefs,
and future, it's time to let go. It's the first step to becoming free
and finding healing in the midst of your storms.

*"Commit your work to the LORD, and your plans will be
established."* (Proverbs 16:3 ESV)

Sometimes we forget we are not the captain, we're the ship. A
ship cannot steer itself. We can have plans, vision, and dreams.
In fact, the true captain counts on it. He loves it when we dream
and plan. He cannot steer a ship that is anchored or moored to the
pier. In order for Him to steer the ship, the ship must be moving.

Yes, I know sometimes we hear poorly or only what we want to
hear, and we head off in directions God never intended for us to
go. He is not intimidated by our mistakes and failures. In fact,
as we'll discuss later, His Spirit is activated when we take risks
and pursue our dreams. When He is given the helm, He will
establish the path our plans take. When we're moving, even if
it's in the wrong direction, which will happen, He is able to "right
the ship" if He is at the helm. Remember, "Man makes plans in

his heart, but God directs his steps."

We make plans, God steers the ship. Let Him take the helm.

Did you know?

Our attempts to control our environment are simply nothing more than a lack of faith. When we lack faith, we are essentially stating we don't believe in God's goodness. He is either good or He is not. There is no middle ground. If He is good, then He is faithful—all the time. If He is faithful, then He should be in control of everything in your life. Don't leave Him outside, let Him steer every aspect of who you are and what you do.

"Things may not be logical or fair, but when God is directing
the events of our lives, they are right."

~ Luci Swindoll

(Best-selling author and speaker)

Prayer

Dear Heavenly Father,

I'm afraid to let go. Yet, in this moment, I say the words, "take the helm." I'm tired of leading and being in control. I relinquish my need to steer, and I trust you to take me where I need to be; wherever that might lead. Again Lord, I surrender. Continue to give me dreams, visions, and excitement for the future, but I will let you lead me, even when it takes me away from my expected outcomes. You are my Lord, and you are my captain. I love you.

In the name of Jesus, Amen.

IT'S MORE THAN I CAN HANDLE

*"God will often give you more than you can handle so you can
learn to depend on Him rather than on yourself."*

~ Craig Groeschel

*(Senior pastor of Life.Church,
bestselling author, and podcast host)*

PULLING BACK THE VEIL

I'm sitting in front of my computer, realizing I'm completely out of my element. This is the first book I've ever tried to write, but since I've "written" most of my life through journaling, I figured, "What can be so hard? I can handle this."

Part of living a lifestyle where we try to be in control of everything comes the ridiculous idea we can handle anything thrown at us. We never want to admit something is "more than we can handle." Actually, many of us feel that would be downright unchristian. It would show a great lack of faith and reveal that when the veil is pulled back, we're all just weak and fragile, and struggle in our trust of God. Who wants to admit to that?

Stress, struggles, frustrations, disappointment, grief, pain, and loss...they are all part of life and will be experienced at some level by everyone. However, sometimes it comes to a point where it feels (and maybe is) overwhelming and more than we can endure. How can this be? Doesn't God promise us He will not give us more than we can bear or handle? Didn't we decide to follow Christ because we wanted a better life? You know, "*shadow of His wings*" and all that. We're supposed to be protected, sheltered, and happy, right? If that's true, then why all the pain, loss, and disappointment?

WHAT IS WRONG WITH ME?

I grew up hearing and believing that God would NEVER give me more than I could handle. Consequently, when I would face issues or situations way over my head and abilities, emotionally and mentally, I would think something must be wrong with me— I'm weak. I'm not a good Christian. I've got a lot more growing to do (okay that last one is still true). What a bunch of bologna (or malarkey, depending on where you're from)!

I've spent most of my life "handling" things way out of my abilities and failing through most of them. Through it all, I've been stretched in my faith, built up in my strength, and I've grown in maturity. That's how God works. That's how He makes us into men and women of destiny and purpose, able to handle more weight and pressure; by putting us in situations or taking advantage of situations we've put ourselves in that are simply too much.

There is an old idiom that says, "A smooth sea never made a skilled sailor" and Bill Hybels, founding pastor of Willow Creek Community Church in Illinois, put it this way, "Storms draw something out of us that calm seas don't."[6] I think the disciples would agree with those statements. As sailors and fishermen, they found themselves in storms that even they couldn't handle; and then Jesus showed up.

"On the same day, when evening had come, He said to them, 'Let us cross over to the other side.' Now when they had left the multitude, they took Him along in the boat as He was. And other little boats were also with Him. And a great windstorm arose, and the waves beat into the boat, so that it was already filling. But He was in the stern, asleep on a pillow. And they awoke Him and said to Him, 'Teacher, do You not care that we are perishing?' Then He arose and rebuked the wind, and said to the sea, 'Peace, be still!' And the wind ceased and there was a great calm. But He said to them, 'Why are you so fearful? How is it that you have no faith?' And they feared exceedingly, and said to one another, 'Who can this be, that even the wind and the sea obey Him!'" (Mark 4:35-41 NKJV)

What would have happened if the disciples had just stayed the course and not said anything? I have to believe they would have arrived safely on the other side. Jesus was in the boat, and He was not concerned—He was sound asleep on a pillow.

What happens in these stormy seasons, if we don't jump ship, is that we see God's faithfulness. It's not that we become strong enough to handle the problem on our own, but we learn He can handle anything, He can calm the seas or He can get us through the storms. In those moments, our faith grows stronger. We learn we can sleep and rest, trusting He is good and will see us through.

WHERE DOES IT SAY THAT?

The truth is the Bible never actually says God won't give us more than we can handle, despite the number of sermons preached in favor of it.

That verse is often misquoted and misunderstood. The actual verse from Paul's first letter to the Corinthians says, *"No temptation has overtaken you that is not common to man. God is faithful, and he will not let you be tempted beyond your ability, but with the temptation he will also provide the way of escape, that you may be able to endure it."* (I Corinthians 10:13 ESV)

Paul is not discussing disappointments or suffering in this verse, he's addressing temptation. Being *"tempted* beyond your ability" and *"being given more than you can handle"* are two distinct and different things.

In fact, when Paul does address despair and afflictions, in his second letter to the Corinthians, he writes this:

"For we do not want you to be unaware, brothers, of the affliction we experienced in Asia. For we were so utterly burdened beyond our strength that we despaired of life itself. Indeed, we felt that we had received the sentence of death. But that was to make us rely not on ourselves but on God who raises the dead." (II Corinthians 1:8-9 ESV)

They were "burdened beyond" what they could do in their strength; to the point they thought they would die. That doesn't sound like "God will never give you more than you can handle."

That being said, did you catch that last part of the verse? "But that was to make us rely not on ourselves but on God who raises the dead." Paul added the "raises the dead" comment as a reminder of the fullness of God's power. We serve the creator of the universe who raises the dead. Are our problems really too big for Him?

Michelle and I have served in the nation of Turkey for seventeen years. Our four children were raised there, and the two youngest were born in Turkey. In February of 2020, God began to speak to us that it was time to relocate our ministry to the United States. It was a difficult decision to make because it required us to leave our home, our church, friends, and ministry family. All of our children's best friends are there, so when I say it was difficult, that is an understatement.

However, we've spent our lives following Him, even when it was difficult. We began making the arrangements, and less than five months after making that very difficult decision, our twenty-year old daughter passed away. Our lives were turned upside down "beyond our strength that we despaired of life itself."

It was more than we could handle. Plain and simple. Our strength failed us, and we were sliding into the dark.

That's when we started trying to wake Jesus up in the stern of our boat. Certainly He must have been asleep. How could a loving God allow this to happen? How could we follow Him with such passion and determination only to find ourselves "*unprotected*" and "*disappointed*"? How could we continue to pursue Him if we could not be certain He would uphold His side of the bargain?

It's because of these inevitable questions that Paul starts verse 8 with *"For we do not want you to be unaware...."* It's important to remember God did not promise we could write our own story where we are never disappointed or unhappy. It's also important to remember we still have an enemy. His plan is simple—to kill, steal, and destroy. One day, we will be free from pain, loss, and disappointment; but not today. Yet, God in His goodness, takes the weight and burdens we *cannot* bear and uses them to drive us into His arms; *"But this happened that we might not rely on ourselves but on God, who raises the dead."* (II Corinthians 1:9 ESV)

We're not supposed to "handle it," *He is.* It's not weakness when we find ourselves in our closets "losing it" and snot-crying into our pillows. It's not weakness when our strength fails us and we say, "I can't do this Lord, please take it and do the miraculous." That's exactly where He wants us to be; in a place of weakness in complete surrender and reliance on Him.

OUR WEAKNESS, HIS STRENGTH

It's in our weakness that He is able to show His strength.

Paul gives a great testimony as an illustration of this very point:

> *"So to keep me from becoming conceited because of the surpassing greatness of the revelations, a thorn was given me in the flesh, a messenger of Satan to harass me, to keep me from becoming conceited. Three times I pleaded with the Lord about this, that it should leave me. But he said to me, 'My grace is sufficient for you, for my power is made perfect in weakness.' Therefore I will boast all the more gladly of my weaknesses, so that the power of Christ may rest upon me. For the sake of Christ, then, I am content with weaknesses, insults, hardships, persecutions, and calamities. For when I am weak, then I am strong."* (II Corinthians 12:7-10 ESV)

19th Century Pastor and Author Charles Spurgeon said this, "The strong are not always vigorous, the wise not always ready, the brave not always courageous, and the joyous not always happy. There may be here and there men of iron, to whom wear and tear work no perceptible detriment, but surely the rust frets even these; and as for ordinary men, the Lord knows, and makes them to know, that they are but dust."[7]

We like to compare our lives and our abilities to what we perceive others to be like. But you see, He is the only one who can raise dead dreams and hopes, making them into something better. No one is able, within themselves, to calm the storms.

He will use every circumstance and every tragedy in our lives to reveal to us our weaknesses; that we might become more faithful to Him and reliant on Him.

At the writing of this book, Michelle and I have not seen the *fullness* of His resurrection power over our most recent pain and loss; but we are learning to give it to Him. We need to learn it, though, because there will be more stress, struggles, frustrations, disappointment, grief, pain, and loss this side of eternity.

It is vital we understand this, because what we learn with each step will help us to take the next one.

Isn't that what life is, taking the next step? One foot in front of the other, trusting in His ability and not our own.

Christian author, speaker, and missionary, Elisabeth Elliot, put it this way, "When you don't know what to do, do what's in front of you."[8] We just keep pushing forward, trusting in the hand of God to handle those things we can't, because, honestly, life is more than we can handle.

BEARING ONE ANOTHER'S BURDENS

There are days when everything seems to come crashing down on me; friends and family we've left behind in our adopted country, readjusting to life and culture in the United States after being away for seventeen years, and, of course the most difficult, the loss of our daughter. Any one of these things alone would be difficult and overwhelming, but having to carry the weight of all of them at the same time has been more than we can handle.

When I stop to think about all we've lost in the past year, the weight of it can press me to a point where I can't seem to find the strength to lift it. The air around me becomes thick to the point I can't breathe. It drives me to the realization I need help. I can't do this alone.

The reality is no one is capable of carrying that weight alone. Even the strongest among us will eventually succumb to the overwhelming pressure that disappointment and loss will bring. That's when we need community, the body of Christ. That's why Paul exhorts the church in Galatians 6:2 with, *"Bear one another's burdens, and so fulfill the law of Christ."*

What is the law of Christ? Jesus tells the disciples in John 15:12-13 ESV,

*"This is my commandment, that you love one another as
I have loved you. Greater love has no one than this, that
someone lay down his life for his friends."*

Michelle and I would not have been able to find our footing
without those who came around us and laid down their lives in
our greatest season of need. We didn't just have the encouraging
Facebook and email messages to get us through. We had friends
who sat with us through it all. People who put their lives on hold,
drove for hours, stayed in a hotel and intentionally focused on us
and our family with no time limits or expectations. Everything
else became secondary as they served us, ministered to us, and
loved us in this season; and continue to do so. This is how the
body functions, and this is why Paul says every part is important.

If you don't have a church family, I encourage you to find one…
being in community starts there. That's why Paul encourages the
church to *"not forsake the fellowship of the saints."* (Hebrews 10:25)
We need each other. We need deep connections, not just surface ones.
Staying the course and getting back on track requires a lot of help.

Here's the kicker—it's a two-way street. You can't have depth in
a community when it is always one person doing all the giving and
sacrificing. We have to lay our lives down for one another. That's
where intimacy is developed and grown. It's not something that
happens overnight, rather, it's living in the trenches with people,
helping to clean up the messes, as well as celebrating the victories.
This is where trust and honor are formed. This is where we can
show others we "have their backs."

When community is established, when dark times come, and
they will, you know you have an army at your back, and you can
face whatever the enemy tries to throw at you. Stay connected.

Did you know?

The Word of God never says your Heavenly Father will not give you more than you can handle. In fact, as we've learned, you are instructed to "count it all joy...when you meet trials of various kinds...." You will have seasons in life where you'll have struggles and disappointments. Period. There is no escape from that. But in your weakness, He is strong. He will show Himself faithful if you will stay the course and keep moving forward.

> "Our vision is so limited we can hardly imagine a love that
> does not show itself in protection from suffering.... The love
> of God did not protect His own Son.... He will not necessarily
> protect us – not from anything it takes to make us like His Son.
> A lot of hammering and chiseling and purifying by fire will
> have to go into the process."
>
> ~ **Elisabeth Elliot**
>
> *(Christian author, speaker, and missionary)*

Prayer

Dear Heavenly Father,

I'm a wreck. This is more than I can handle. I've tried to carry it on my own, but I'm collapsing under the weight of it. I need you. Your Word says it's in my weakness that you are strongest. Well, I'm weak right now, and I need your strength. Come Holy Spirit and fill in my gaps. Be my strength in this season of my life that YOU will get glory from it and others will be attracted to your healing power and strength. I love you.

In Jesus' name I pray, Amen.

5

THE DWELLING PLACE

*"The man who has made God his dwelling place
will always have a safe habitation."*

~ A.W. Tozer

(American Christian pastor, author, and theologian)

LIVING IN THE PAIN

Needless to say, 2020 was a struggle for our family (and many others). "Struggle" seems like a watered down version of what we have actually gone through. We feel shattered and incomplete. Unrecognizable. I was under the impression "time heals all wounds" and I would be significantly better today than I was yesterday. Not true.

I'm discovering there are stages of "goodbye." I'm not just saying goodbye to Aly; I'm saying goodbye to all the hopes, dreams, and expectations I had for her life. There were a lot of those.

Shortly after her "Celebration of Life," we had the unenviable and extremely difficult job of packing up her apartment and moving all of her things into our new home; another goodbye. Before this book is finished, we will celebrate her twenty-first birthday and the one year anniversary of her death. The opportunities to say goodbye never seem to end.

I don't know what the future holds or what new or tragic disappointments await me, but I know I don't want to always be peeking around corners wondering what's coming next.

When we dwell on our pain and disappointments, we create an expectancy in our lives we can't ever escape, and we move from one crisis to another.

Through the process, I'm learning there is a fine line between remembering and dwelling. Yes, I absolutely must take time to remember Aly—who she was, what she did and the joy she took in living life and loving people. There is healing in that. However, I cannot allow myself to camp or dwell there.

A "dwelling" is a place where we live. So, when we use "dwell" in reference to our thoughts, we are literally talking about places where we choose to live in our minds and emotions.

When I dwell on my circumstances, struggles, or pain, I give Satan an opportunity to pull me into the depths of grief and lock me into a room of despair, discouragement, pain, and self-loathing. Make no mistake, it will become my home; a place where I live, breathe, eat, and sleep. It actually will become more like a prison cell, a place that is difficult to escape.

Several years ago some things happened in one of our close ministry relationships. Without going into detail, the relationship was broken and it left us reeling. We were completely caught off guard by the circumstances, and it hurt deeply.

We never had really walked through this level of broken relationship before, and we handled it poorly. We allowed offense to set in and we began to dwell on the situation. It consumed everything—our thoughts, our conversations, our family, even our marriage. It took us several years to get through that completely, because we set up camp, making the problem and resulting pain our home. It locked us in a prison cell, and almost destroyed our marriage and our ministry. It wasn't the broken relationship that did that, rather, it was because we couldn't release it to God. It was more than we could handle, so we shouldn't have tried. Instead, we made it our dwelling place.

John 15 is the well-known chapter about the vine and the vine dresser. In verses 4 - 10 Jesus talks to His disciples about "abiding in Him."

"Abide in me, and I in you. As the branch cannot bear fruit by itself, unless it abides in the vine, neither can you, unless you abide in me." (John 15:4 ESV)

"As the Father has loved me, so have I loved you. Abide in my love. If you keep my commandments, you will abide in my love, just as I have kept my Father's commandments and abide in his love." (John 15: 9-10 ESV)

The word John chooses to use here for "abide" is the Greek word *meno.* It means to stay in a given place, remain, dwell. It's where we live, where we take up residence.

Jesus is telling His disciples that in order to have fruitful, productive lives for the Kingdom of God, they must find their permanence in Him. He must be their dwelling place.

The message is obviously not just for the twelve disciples. He's speaking to any of us who call ourselves followers of Jesus. Our dwelling place should be in Him. Our thoughts, emotions, plans, hurts, and disappointments...everything must be in Him, given to Him.

These are some of the Lord's final words to His followers, His friends. He is about to leave them and He needs them to understand a few very important things. One of the most important issues He chooses to discuss is this command to "abide." The importance of this discussion was lost on the disciples in that moment, but Jesus knew they would need these words to get through the "shattering" that was coming.

To put an exclamation point on His words, He concludes the discussion about abiding with these words, *"These things I have spoken to you, that My joy may remain in you, and that your joy may be full."* (John 15:11 NKJV)

Did you see that? "...that my joy may *remain* in you...." It's that word *meno* again. "That my joy may *ABIDE/DWELL in you."* The promise is when we abide or dwell in Him, His joy will then live and dwell in us!

Now, consider that statement in relationship to the verse in James 1, "Count it all joy, my brothers, when you meet trials of various kinds...." How do we count it all joy? By abiding in Him! By dwelling on Him and His goodness, His joy lives in us!

Notice He didn't say "...so that your problems will go away" or "...so that people will treat you better." He said, "...that your joy may be full." It's not the temporal joy you have when your problems disappear, it's the eternal joy always with you, in the good times and in the middle of the storm. When He takes up residence in our lives, so does His joy. You get the fullness of who He is: Love. Joy. Peace.

The problem is we only want Him to be a part of our lives when it's convenient, when it doesn't interfere with other things and other plans.

I'm sorry to disappoint you, but it doesn't work that way. That's not what "dwelling" means. It's not a "come and go" relationship. He gives us His fullness, His joy abides or dwells in us when we dwell in Him. It's an exchange, but it's not an "I'll give you whatever you give me" exchange. It's a "you give me your everything, and I'll give you my everything" exchange.

Trust me, we're getting the better deal, but it is all or nothing. We don't get to keep some things back and expect God will still give us His fullness.

It really is all or nothing.

To illustrate this point, Jesus said these words to the church in Laodicea, *"I know your works: you are neither cold nor hot. Would that you were either cold or hot! So, because you are lukewarm, and neither hot nor cold, I will spit you out of my mouth."* (Revelation 3:15-16 ESV)

If we're going to dwell somewhere, it's a place of permanence, a place of commitment and community. We can't have our feet in two "dwelling places" and expect to develop community. The same applies to the Kingdom of God. We can't call ourselves citizens of the kingdom while living in, or like, the world. We have to choose.

Dwelling on your problems, disappointment, or loss will bring nothing but a prison cell of more pain and grief. However, making Jesus your dwelling place brings fullness of joy in spite of the disappointment and pain.

Again, this doesn't promise the pain will go away or you'll forget the circumstances that brought the pain. Actually it's vital we remember the past because we learn from our failures, pain, and disappointments as we dwell in Jesus and on His kingdom and the plans He has for us. It's a bright future full of hope and peace.

Aly's favorite Scripture was Jeremiah 29:11, *"For I know the plans I have for you, declares the Lord, plans for welfare and not for evil, to give you a future and a hope."*

We have that Scripture posted everywhere to remind us of our future, and that it's full of hope. Our dwelling place is in Him, not in our pain, loss, and disappointment.

Many of the Psalms talk about dwelling in the presence of the Lord:

"How lovely is your dwelling place,
  O LORD of hosts!
My soul longs, yes, faints
  for the courts of the LORD;

my heart and flesh sing for joy
to the living God....
For a day in your courts is better
than a thousand elsewhere.
I would rather be a doorkeeper in the house of my God
than dwell in the tents of wickedness." (Psalm 84: 1-2, 10 ESV)

"Surely the righteous shall give thanks to your name;
the upright shall dwell in your presence." (Psalm 140:13 NKJV)

"He who dwells in the shelter of the Most High will abide in
the shadow of the Almighty." (Psalm 91:1 ESV)

When pain and disappointment find their mark in our lives, we can take shelter in the courts of the Lord, our strong tower and a shelter from the storms.

WHAT IF?

We also must be constantly aware when we allow the questions of "what if?" to dwell in our thoughts. It tends to occur when our stories have an unforeseen plot change; when our expectations don't match our outcome. "What if we had done 'this' or 'that' differently?"

I have played the "what if" game. What if Aly had stayed in California and never moved to Texas? What if we had brought her home to Turkey for a visit earlier than we were planning? The one I've battled with the most is, "What if I had just been there to protect her?"

When we start going down the "what if" road, we play into the hands of the enemy. We allow him to lead us to a "dwelling place" where we will have a difficult time escaping.

Many times, the "what if's" turn into blaming and self-loathing. I still have to guard my heart against that from time to time.

In the winter of 2019-20, we were in the United States for four months. Our two oldest were attending Bethel's School of Supernatural Ministry in California, and we had just transitioned our church overseas to our local associate pastors, precious Turkish friends. We felt it would be good to spend some time away and visit our kids, friends, and family in the United States while also giving the new pastors some time to lead without us looking over their shoulders. While we were in the states, the Lord began to speak to me about expanding our ministry and the need to move back to the United States for that to happen.

We weren't excited about that possibility, but we agreed to pray about it. We returned to our adopted country of Turkey at the end of February and, of course, began to go into COVID lockdowns in March. During the time of quarantine, God began to confirm to us that we were to transition back to the states.

When we told Aly, she was both excited and sad…excited she would be closer to her mom and dad, sad because she still considered Turkey to be her home. She had been offered an internship with a ministry in Dallas, where we considered moving, and that was a confirmation to her that she should take the offer more seriously.

Aly took the internship and moved to Dallas in May, and we made the decision to transition to the states in September. Everyone was sad, but excited about this new season in our lives. On July 5, on our way to church to share with the congregation about the changes coming, we found out Aly had been in an accident, the one that eventually took her life.

It's amazing how quickly everything can change, and with that, how quickly the "what if's" begin to enter your mind. Then comes the blaming. Did I miss God? Did I set all of this in motion? Am I to blame? Is all of this my fault?

In most instances, we can't change the outcome by wondering what we could've done differently. Regardless, we often choose in that moment to focus and dwell on the "what if's" of the past instead of the potential of the future.

Instead, we should ask: What if things turn out better than I imagined? What if God does something amazing and unexpected? What if I put my trust in the only One who can see the beginning from the end and everything in between?

When our "what if's" are placed in the mighty and capable hands of the Father, they become hopes, not wishes. Hope brings life, joy, and peace.

One of our "what if's" we've placed in the hands of God was a dream our daughter Aly had. From as early as we can remember, Aly loved horses. She had books, pictures, and drawings of every horse imaginable. The vision the Lord gave her was to one day own an equine therapy ranch. She wanted to use horses to reach troubled and handicapped youth and individuals suffering from trauma, abuse, or PTSD. So, we asked the Lord, "What if you let us fulfill her vision?" That "what if" has put us on a journey to find a way to incorporate what we are already doing to reach the nations with Aly's dream.

What if we turned our hopelessness around and dwelt on Him and His plans? If we do that, it will put us on unexpected journeys; journeys that become God inspired and God redeemed.

What if? It's a great question to ask when we direct it toward the only One who can answer it. We can't dwell on the past, we can only learn from it and let God develop our future in a way that brings victory from the depths of disappointment.

THE NEXT STEP

Our family is in an in-between place right now. Having just moved back to the states after sixteen years in another country, we are now looking for our own home. We've been blessed to stay in the beautiful home of another family while they are overseas, but we know it's temporary. We need a home, a place to "dwell."

However, someone else is not going to choose our home for us. We have to make that choice. The same applies to our emotional, mental, and spiritual dwelling places. Where we live is a choice we have to make. Sometimes it's a difficult one, but it is still a choice.

> *"And if it is evil in your eyes to serve the LORD, choose this day whom you will serve, whether the gods your fathers served in the region beyond the River, or the gods of the Amorites in whose land you dwell. **But as for me and my house, we will serve the LORD.**"* (Joshua 24:15 ESV)

Notice how Joshua says "...choose this day..." This will be your single most important lesson in life...every day is a choice whom you will serve. You can blame it on your circumstances or other people, but ultimately it comes down to your choice and whom you will serve; where you will dwell.

You may have been given a "bum rap" and have fallen into your current situation. You may have been treated poorly and genuinely suffered at the hands of others. Yet, whether you will get up and go home is entirely your responsibility...no one else's. Will you remain a victim or become the victor? It's all about choices.

As for me, Michelle, and our house, His courts are where we choose to dwell, this is where we choose to live. We will remember our pain and the suffering it took to make us who we are, but we will not dwell there. We choose Him.

Did you know?

A home is more than just a place we visit, it's where you laugh, cry, grow, and mature. However, if we choose to lock ourselves away in a cell of pain, self-pity, and disappointment, we will never get through the hurt, despair, or hopelessness associated with it. To choose to dwell in His presence and courts of praise is to invite

His fullness into our lives. His joy and His peace will abide in us, even in the midst of the storms.

> "A believer may pass through much affliction, and yet secure very little blessing from it all. Abiding in Christ is the secret of securing all that the Father meant the chastisement to bring us."
> ### ~ Andrew Murray
> *(South African writer, teacher, and Christian pastor)*

Prayer

Dear Heavenly Father,

I've dwelt in many places, but none of them have brought me peace or joy. I've tasted of your goodness, but I want to dine at your table. I choose this day to abide in you! Better is one day in your courts than a thousand elsewhere! Teach me how to remain in your presence and fill me with the fullness of your joy. I love you.

In the mighty name of Jesus I pray, amen.

CHOICES

"Our lives are fashioned by our choices. First we make our choices. Then our choices make us."

~ Anne Frank

(Jewish Holocaust victim who gained fame posthumously with The Diary of a Young Girl)

IT IS WHAT IT IS

If we're being real, most of us would admit to wanting the end of a situation or circumstance to be easier than the beginning. After all, that's the way it is supposed to be when we decide to follow Jesus, right? We didn't get into this thing for our crappy lives to continue being crappy. So why hasn't it changed? Why hasn't it gotten better? What are we doing wrong?

Our journey through life is full of twists and turns, and it always comes down to *choices*.

When James says, *"Consider it nothing but joy, my brothers and sisters, whenever you fall into various trials,"* he is making a statement about choices. The word "Consider" is "hegiomai" in Greek. One of its meanings is "to lead or to govern." What James is trying to communicate to the church is we have to *lead and govern* ourselves toward joy and rejoicing, toward a correct attitude.

Let's look at James' statement again,

> *"Consider it nothing but joy, my brothers and sisters,*
> *whenever you fall into various trials...."*

Notice the wording, "Whenever you FALL into various trials..." Sometimes our "trials" are self-inflicted, the result of our poor choices and actions, but sometimes we "fall" into suffering, pain, and disappointment. We didn't do anything wrong, and our choices didn't necessarily put us there. Yet, because of our circumstances, we find ourselves in a pit of despair. This was our situation with Aly. I beat myself up trying to consider all the things I could've done to have prevented this from happening. I even went down that dark path of wondering, "Am I being judged for my poor choices?" It's human nature to begin looking for the cause or the reason. If we can figure that out, maybe we can fix it. Sometimes, the ugly but simple truth is, "It is what it is."

LEADING OURSELVES

Notice James doesn't say, "We fall into joy." He doesn't say, "Hey, don't worry, just keep walking and you'll stumble your way into happiness." That's because that will never happen. We will never "fall" into a proper response to our troubles. Instead, we must "lead, govern, choose" how to respond to them. Joy does not just "fall" on us. Suffering, pain, disappointments...these things may "fall on us," meaning, many times, disappointments are out of our control.

However, joy and rejoicing are choices always in our control. We have to lead and govern ourselves well, especially during times and seasons of disappointment.

When Michelle and I returned from the funeral home after a very painful time of making all the decisions for Aly's burial, we were a wreck. Looking at the different plots, headstones, and flowers, and making the arrangements for the church and funeral service was one of the most difficult moments in our lives. However, after making it back to our Airbnb, I made a difficult choice—I put my headphones on, went to the bedroom, and worshiped.

It was not easy because nothing in that moment made sense. Emotionally I was a mess, and truthfully, I was still mad at God. Yet, in my heart, I knew He was good. I knew He was faithful. So, I *chose* to worship. I didn't wait until I felt like worshiping, because, honestly, several months later, I still don't "feel" like worshiping most days. I have to lead myself into a place of worship.

I find myself, every day, having to make a choice. There have been many days I've chosen poorly. It's okay. There's been grace for that. Yet, I can't make that my new lifestyle. It's difficult, but God is after something. He's after transformation. His goal is to make me like Jesus.

I'm uncertain where I heard this quote, but I wrote it down a long time ago, and it has been a reminder to me every time I've felt knocked down and beat up, "You don't die by falling into the river, you die by staying submerged."

A lot of the time we fall into the river and just lay there, face down and defeated.

There are days when you have fallen into something and you have to decide to get up. You have to lead yourself in that decision.

When it comes to worship, joy, peace, or any other positive Godly emotion, sometimes you have to act yourself into a feeling rather than feeling yourself into an action. If we keep waiting on the feelings, we will continue to lay in the river, submerged.

By the end of my time of worship that day, I found joy, peace and His presence. Don't get me wrong, I was still a wreck...honestly, I still am. That's what is so beautiful about His presence. **He is at His best in the midst of the storm.**

TALK TO YOURSELF

David understood this better than anyone. He fell into a lot of problems, and unfortunately, many of his problems were self-inflicted, caused by his poor choices. However, he knew how to lead himself out of the pit. Psalm 42 is an excellent example of how we do this.

> *"Why are you cast down, O my soul,*
> *and why are you in turmoil within me?*
> *Hope in God; for I shall again praise him,*
> *my salvation and my God.*
> *My soul is cast down within me;*
> *therefore I remember you*
> *from the land of Jordan and of Hermon,*
> *from Mount Mizar."* (Psalm 42:5-6 ESV)

I love it. David is literally talking to himself (So I'm in good company). However, it's not just idle chatter. David is intentional in his message. He encourages himself. He says, "Hey David! Why are you so down? Hope in God, praise Him! Remember what He has done in your life! He is faithful!

I want to stop here for a minute because it's important to note God did not create suffering. It's easy to fall into that trap of "God has a reason for this." Nope. God did not "take" my daughter because it was "just her time to go" or because "He just loved her so much He couldn't be away from her any longer."

These statements, and others like them, are nothing more than man's attempt to explain something we have no capacity to understand. *New York Times* best-selling author, Bob Goff, put it this way, "God doesn't break things so He can fix them; He fixes broken things so He can use them."[9]

Trials, persecution, pain, and suffering may "fall" on us, but not because God caused it. The reality is we live in a broken world among broken things. Consequently, things in our lives break, and suffering, trials, and pain happen to all of us.

However, while God may not have created our places of disappointment and pain, He will use those moments and seasons in our lives to bring us into maturity and Godly character. Our reactions to these moments will either produce joy and peace or more suffering and pain. That choice is placed squarely on our shoulders.

TWO INVITATIONS, ONE CHOICE

Making a choice to rejoice, when something in our life breaks, is not easy— especially when we allow grief to become our comfort rather than the thing that drives us to become better. Maybe I'm different, but sometimes when I walk through difficulties and disappointment, I look for the comfort of the pain. I look to wrap myself in the darkness.

That sounds strange when I say it out loud, but in that moment of grief and hurt, it seems warm, inviting, and comfortable. It's the enemy's invitation to pull me toward despair and hopelessness, and to steal my sacrifice. On the surface, it looks inviting, but in reality it's a place of darkness and pain. I know. I've been there...I am there. Every day. Staring down into that pit and making the decision, the choice, to rejoice. The sacrifice is mine. Satan cannot have it.

There is a famous quote by Sitting Bull, a Native American chief who lived in the 19th century. He is attributed to saying, "Inside of me there are two dogs. One is mean and evil, and the other is good, and they fight each other all the time. When asked which one wins, I answer, the one I feed the most."

So there are two invitations at play. An invitation to despair and hopelessness and an invitation to a table of intimacy where there is peace and joy. The one we CHOOSE to feed will determine the one we serve.

It's upside down, backwards. It makes no sense. How can I rejoice while I'm hurting so much? How can my pain ever become the place of my greatest victory?

It's the mystery that is God. It's the "not yet" of His kingdom at work in my "now" situation. It does not make sense, but it is the truth of my worst pain; it can and should become a place of victory.

James says in Chapter 4, *"Draw near to God, and He will draw near to you."* It's an action that begins a chain reaction from the kingdom down to Earth. The first step is always drawing near to Him.

It's not magic. It also doesn't suddenly make all the pain go away. However, it does begin to build something within me called "endurance," the place of constancy. On that foundation of "no quit," God can begin to build other things like character and hope. When that structure has strength, it can bear up under the intense pressure of suffering and pain.

Pastor and Author John Ortberg, in his book *Eternity is Now in Session*, writes, "Salvation isn't about getting you into heaven; it's about getting heaven into you. It's not about relocation; it's about transformation. It's not about what God wants to do *to* you; it's about what God wants to do *in* you. It's about allowing Jesus' kingdom life to permeate our little lives one moment, one choice at a time."[10]

It always begins with a choice to move forward. Having endurance is not simply saying "I will not quit." It's doing the right things to position yourself for a lifestyle of staying the course. Some of those things are going to be tough and require a lot of humility. That's why the kingdom must get *in* you.

Jesus Himself said it like this, *"I have said these things to you, that in me you may have peace. In the world you will have tribulation. But take heart; I have overcome the world."* (John 16:33)

"In me you may have peace." IN ME. Again, there is this choice, this action. It invites us to wrap ourselves in the ONLY thing that can truly bring comfort, warmth, peace, and joy...His presence.

The other invitation is a lie of the enemy that has been couched in laziness and the easy road. However, it's actually the road that leads to destruction and more pain. It seems warm and inviting at first, but the end of that road leads to a dark pit of despair, disappointment, and depression. Once you're in that pit, it's cold, lonely, and difficult to climb out of.

> *"There is a way that seems right to a man, but its end is the way to death."* (Proverbs 14:12)

Choices.

It's difficult to choose joy. I know. I'm at that crossroads every day. Some days I make the wrong choice, so I know from experience how deep that pit can go, and how cold and dark it actually is.

> *"Finally, brothers, whatever is true, whatever is honorable, whatever is just, whatever is pure, whatever is lovely, whatever is commendable, if there is any excellence, if there is anything worthy of praise, think about these things."* (Philippians 4:8)

Choices.

I choose HIM. I choose Joy. I choose Life. And I choose HIS kingdom, not this one.

Did you know?

You have the authority to lead yourself into joy and peace. It's not a magic word or phrase, rather it's an action, a choice to walk in His joy and His peace. Our lives are full of daily choices, and those choices will lead us to one of two places—the presence of God or the pit of despair. There is nothing or no one that can change your circumstances or attitude. Only you can do that. However, your Heavenly Father is drawn toward those who draw near to Him. Choose Him.

"Every choice you make has an end result."

~ Zig Ziglar

(American author, salesman, and motivational speaker)

Prayer

Dear Heavenly Father,

Most of my life I've looked to things as a solution to my pain and disappointment, and I have struggled to find joy and to find peace. They have failed me every, single time. This time, I choose you. I choose your joy and your peace. I will lead myself into a better way of thinking and a better attitude. I can do this because your joy is IN ME—YOU are in me! I love you.

In Jesus precious name, amen.

A LOSS OF MOTIVATION

"Success is not final; failure is not fatal: it is the courage to continue that counts."

~Winston Churchill
(Prime Minister of the United Kingdom, 1940 to 1945 and 1951 to 1955)

DOES IT REALLY MATTER?

The fact that I was able to write a book during the worst season of grief and disappointment in my life is a testimony to the importance of choices. Because, like it or not, finding motivation in seasons of discouragement and disappointment requires making decisions every day to move forward.

As the chapter suggests, through my grief journey, I've greatly struggled in the area of motivation. I told you much of this book would be raw, and that is just the raw truth; many of the things we are discussing, I'm still working through.

In this process, I've found it difficult to find the motivation to "do." Of course, writing this book has been helpful and has given me a venue to flush out some of these thoughts. However, I still find many days when I wake up, I feel, right out of the gate, I've hit a wall. Early in the process, I struggled to get myself out of bed, and that's never been a problem for me as I've never been a late sleeper. Yet, the mornings were difficult. It was another day I had to face my grief and pain. As I slowly began to find victory over my mornings, I found that I still struggled to get anything done. I just wasn't motivated. Everything had lost its flavor and purpose.

I think that was a big issue—purpose. It's not that I *lost* my purpose, I just couldn't find the value in it. Why am I doing this? What will it achieve? It won't bring my daughter back, so why does it matter? These were questions that constantly plagued my thoughts and actions. Every day was a fight for my desire or motivation to accomplish something.

HE CARES FOR YOU

The problem was I didn't feel like fighting. I didn't want to struggle or compete with my flesh. I just wanted to give up, give in. Yet, I couldn't find peace in that, either, because I knew deep down I have been called to something higher. So, I lived in a constant state of wanting to have value and purpose, but not wanting the struggle that went with choosing every day to keep going.

Peter addresses this in his first letter. He writes:

> *"Therefore humble yourselves under the mighty hand of God, that He may exalt you in due time, casting all your care upon Him, for He cares for you. Be sober, be vigilant; because your adversary the devil walks about like a roaring lion, seeking whom he may devour. Resist him, steadfast in the faith, knowing that the same sufferings are experienced by your brotherhood in the world. But may the God of all grace, who called us to His eternal glory by Christ Jesus, after you have suffered a while, perfect, establish, strengthen, and settle you."* (1 Peter 5:6-10 NKJV)

Peter gives us a great outline to follow. He lists four primary things we need to "do" to get ourselves back on track, to find our motivation and drive again.

First, and possibly the most difficult, is to humble ourselves. We need help. Recognizing we need help is only half the victory. We need to humble ourselves and ask for help.

When you're going through a difficult time, you will be surprised by how many people will understand and offer you help and encouragement. It's vital to surround yourself with people who have your back and will lift your arms when they're tired or when you don't feel like fighting.

We have friends like that. They've been at our sides through this entire ordeal. They have sacrificed, climbed into the pit with us, and helped push us out. They continue to do that. Is it humbling? You better believe it. However, we wouldn't have made it without them. You can't recover without humility. A lack of humility drives us into the arms of independence, the "I can do it on my own, I don't need any help" attitude. It's that attitude that will keep you in the pit and drain you of all strength and motivation.

There is an addition to this first step though; it's the "*that He may exalt you in due time*" addendum. There are seasons when we need to have patience in our humility; allowing Him to lift us up "in due time." Sometimes we just need to rest in Him. We have become a culture of "doing." However, when walking through disappointment, grief, and loss, we need to learn to let Him put us back on track in His timing. That requires patience and a willingness to trust in our heavenly Father to lead us faithfully.

That can be difficult when we find ourselves in a season of disappointment because, much of the time, disappointment leads us to begin questioning God's faithfulness. We have to ignore the rantings of our mind and allow our faith to drive us forward. Faith is staying the course even (or especially) when everything in the natural screams for us to stop and go in a different direction.

The second statement Peter makes is to cast "all your care upon Him, for He cares for you." We need the help of others, but if we do not give everything over to Him, we'll keep returning to the same place we've been trapped in.

I remember in the midst of all of the pain, the Lord spoke to me and asked a simple question: "Do you want to do this or do you want me to do it?" It sounds like a ridiculous question, but I got the message. He is perfectly willing to let me lead, or carry the burden; but I don't need to. However, I do have to give it to Him. He will not take it from me.

So often, I think, we have the expectation He will come in like a knight in shining armor on a white steed and take all our problems from us. That seems like a wonderful fairy tale, but, unfortunately, it doesn't work that way. We have to cast our cares on Him. The actual word in the Greek literally means to throw our anxiety on Him. It implies putting it far away and giving Him charge over the struggles.

Sometimes we say things like, "just let it go," but this verse suggests something a bit more intentional in "*casting all* your care *upon*" the Lord. There is a stronger action involved, not just a "letting go." It's also not just a "casting" but a "casting upon" something. It's intentional. It has purpose. It's directed toward Him.

We don't just throw or cast our cares away, we actually cast or throw them upon Jesus. He wants to carry our burdens because He cares for us!

BE VIGILANT

Third, Peter says to, "Be sober, be vigilant; because your adversary the devil walks about like a roaring lion, seeking whom he may devour." When we are in distress, our vigilance is one of the first things to go. When motivation goes, so does our attention and focus on the things happening around us.

Our enemy, Satan, loves these moments in our lives. He is looking, waiting for them. When he sees them, like a lion, he pounces. That's why it's a struggle, because we have an enemy, and he will take advantage of our every weakness. However, the Word of God says our weakness can be our strength if we are alert and aware of what is going on around us.

> *"Therefore I take pleasure in infirmities, in reproaches, in needs, in persecutions, in distresses, for Christ's sake. For when I am weak, then I am strong."* (2 Corinthians 12:10)

There are practical things that have helped me to stay focused and moving forward. Soon after Aly's death, one thing I tried making myself do every day after I woke up was to make my bed. Okay, I can hear you laughing. I know, it seems like an oversimplification of a larger problem, but I'm telling you it helped. It was a small accomplishment that, at the time, felt like a huge victory. And yes, I continue to do this every day, and with time, it has gotten easier.

It's really about taking the next step and not looking too far down the road. It's always the next step that brings victory and keeps us vigilant. Find and do the "little things" that bring victory and accomplishments. It punches the enemy in the face and says, "I see you prowling around, and I'm not going to be devoured today!"

When we stay vigilant, we give way to the power of the Holy Spirit over our circumstances and emotions. When we can identify the problem, humble ourselves, and cast our cares upon Him, then, in our weakness, He shows Himself strong. He takes our small victories and accomplishments and puts His wind in our sails.

Finally, after humbling ourselves, casting our cares and anxieties on Him and remaining vigilant, then, as Peter states, we can resist. We resist the enemy by remaining steadfast in Him. It's not in our strength that we are resisting, it's in His. But, His strength is activated through our humility, through our choice to involve Him and to stay aware and focused on the enemy's attempts to pull us away from His presence.

These "steps" may seem an oversimplified way of dealing with a lack of motivation that results from disappointment and pain, but the reality is that following Christ is not complicated. We complicate things all on our own because we have a hard time believing our Heavenly Father wants the best for us and has provided a simple solution of obedience to all of our problems, pains, and grief.

STABILITY

One final thought…there is a promise we hold to in 1 Peter 5:10 (ESV), *"And after you have suffered a little while, the God of all grace, who has called you to his eternal glory in Christ, will himself restore, confirm, strengthen, and establish you."*

There are seasons of suffering and struggle, and yet there is an end. We do not have to keep going around the same mountain every day, but it's only if we approach the throne of God and cast our anxieties on Him. If we make a choice to do that, He will perfect us, establish us, strengthen us, and, my favorite, He will "settle" us!

That word for settle actually means to "set fast, fix, to make stable." The inference is HE WILL DO IT! Not you, not your spouse, or your pastor; HE WILL DO IT.

I don't know about you, but my struggles have left me feeling out of balance, off kilter, out of whack. But His promise is that when we've pushed through and stayed the course, He will establish us and set us firmly in a stable place. That's encouraging. I'm looking forward to that day, and I'm beginning to see it.

Depression, discouragement, and grief will try to take us out and destroy our motivation and purpose. If we will stay the course and do not give up, letting Him lead and carry the weight, we will make it through. We will find our purpose again, and it will be better than we ever dreamed.

> *"And let us not grow weary while doing good, for in due season we shall reap if we do not lose heart."*
> *(*Galatians 6:9 NKJV)

Did you know?

Finding your motivation in seasons of disappointment and grief, for most, does not happen overnight. It's a process of making daily decisions to do the little things. Zechariah 4:10 (NLT) says, "Do not despise these small beginnings, for the LORD rejoices to see the work begin...." We are on a journey of healing and restoration. It takes time, so every day make the choice to stay in the fight.

> "Relying on God has to start all over every day,
> as if nothing has yet been done."
> ### ~ C.S. Lewis
> (Lay theologian and British writer)

Prayer

Dear Heavenly Father,

I feel lost. I have no desire to keep going. Nothing makes sense to me anymore. I need you. I can't do this without you. I lay all of today's worries, all of today's fear and all of my pain at your feet. Help me to do the things I need to do today to move forward. I won't worry about tomorrow, just help me with today. I love you. In Jesus name I pray, amen.

ALIGNING OUR EXPECTATIONS WITH HIS TRUTH

"Always God's goodness is the ground of our expectation."

~ A.W. Tozer

ARRIVING AT THE DESTINATION

Making good choices based on who we know God to be is a daily exercise. Research suggests it takes, on average, sixty-six days for a choice or behavior to become a habit. So, making good choices consistently is crucial to developing a healthy *lifestyle* of choices. Forming good habits in difficult seasons depends, consequently, on being faithful in the little things.

Sometimes we think making a good choice, being obedient to the leading of Christ and His word, one or two times is enough. Hoorah, we wave our victory flag and take a vacation to the Bahamas. Whew, check obedience off the list.

It's important we understand there is a difference between obedience and faithfulness. They are not the same thing. Obedience can be applied to a single event, but faithfulness occurs when obedience becomes a lifestyle.

Obedience can also occur as an emotional response to a situation or moment of influence, but faithfulness must be driven by character and integrity, not emotions. If your emotions are the only thing that drives your obedience, your obedience will never mature into faithfulness.

So, character matters. Contrary to popular belief, the ends alone do not always justify the means. The journey and the destination must be in alignment, and the value of the journey is determined by how we arrive at the destination.

As Paul writes in his letter to the Romans,

> *"Not only that, but we rejoice in our sufferings, knowing that suffering produces endurance, and endurance produces character, and character produces hope, and hope does not put us to shame, because God's love has been poured into our hearts through the Holy Spirit who has been given to us."* (Romans 5:3-5 ESV)

These are not simple occurrences Paul refers to in this passage. He's talking about a journey. These are valleys walked through, mountains climbed, and oceans crossed. It's "where the rubber meets the road." It is a journey. Endurance, character, and hope are developed over the course of a lifetime, not in a day or an instant.

Michelle and I would never have been able to handle the extreme grief of losing a child if we had not already walked through valleys, mountains, and oceans of disappointment. God began to build a foundation in our lives years ago as we slowly learned to fully trust Him when things seemed to be falling apart. The reality is grief and disappointment don't get smaller, it's just we get bigger as we journey through life and learn to trust the Lord.

The word Paul uses for "produces" in Romans 5 is the Greek word *katergazomai*. It means to "work fully" or "work out." It's interesting because Paul uses the same word in a letter to the Philippians.

> *"¹² Therefore, my beloved, as you have always obeyed, so now, not only as in my presence but much more in my absence, <u>work out</u> your own salvation with fear and trembling,¹³ for it is God who works in you, both to will and to work for his good pleasure."* (Philippians 2:12-13 ESV)

Once again, Paul is discussing a journey of faithfulness. He says to obey, not only in His presence, but also in His absence. In other words, always. It is a process of *working out* our character and our commitment to the cause of Christ; a journey of discipleship and becoming true followers of Jesus. We didn't reach our destination with a heartfelt prayer of repentance on that wonderful day when we gave our lives to Christ. Rather, we began a journey toward a destination of fellowship and intimacy with our Heavenly Father, which sets us on a journey of faithfulness through consistent obedience.

The journey is important because it's when our character is developed and *worked out* that we can withstand the storms and disappointments of life, stay the course, *and finish well.*

It's when our character is developed that we can rise from our grief, our loss, and even our failures and press on toward the destination Christ has for us. Without character being developed and tested within us, as the Scriptures say, we become people tossed to and fro by every wave (Ephesians 4:14 ESV).

Without endurance producing character, hope has no place to grow. Producing hope in our lives is a process birthed during the journey. Solomon penned it best when he wrote, *"Hope deferred makes the heart sick...."* (Proverbs 13:12a ESV) We need hope, but it is only developed through endurance and character, otherwise it's just a "wish," something with no foundation, function, or substance.

HOW DO WE GET THERE?

So how do we get from the pit of despair to a place of hope? How do we move from simple obedience driven by our emotions and circumstances to a lifestyle of faithfulness that is a stalwart against the storms?

One of the first things we must do is to align our expectations to His truth. Remember? It's what James was trying to say in James 1:2, *"Consider it nothing but joy, my brothers and sisters, **whenever** you fall into various trials."*

He was trying to set our expectations in alignment with the truth of God's Word. Deciding to follow Christ is not an invitation to a life without problems, pain, and suffering. It's an invitation to a life that is still battered, broken, and bruised, but full of love, peace, and joy. It's a victorious life in the midst of the storms! That's why we do as James said and *"consider it ALL joy...."*

Because *"...we know that for those who love God all things work together for good, for those who are called according to his purpose."* (Romans 8:28 ESV)

So, the destination matters and especially how we arrive there. The journey and the destination are equally important. I used to think the journey included a few mountains and valleys and a lot of wide-open plains, where we work and run our race. What I failed to understand is there are also oceans to cross. The mountains can be discouraging just because of their overwhelming size, how they take over the entire landscape, and the closer we get to them, the larger they seem (finances, relationships, and dreams bigger than our abilities).

When we are in the valley, it's easy to get lost and give up hope when we can't see the forest for all the trees (failures, insecurities, and uncertainties). The oceans however, can drown us in despair, depression, disappointment, and grief.

The thing about the oceans is we have nothing solid under our feet. We feel helpless against the wind and waves. It was where the disciples found themselves on a few occasions. Yet, we watch as Peter steps out of the boat, and finds, for a moment of incredible faith, solid footing. It was in the midst of a fierce storm, one that saw veteran fishermen afraid for their lives, that Peter walked on water. We can, too.

God did not calm the sea before calling Peter out of the boat. Peter stepped out anyway. Sometimes it's the Jesus IN the storm that we need when our faith begins to fail.

This is what the journey will teach us, and that is what our Heavenly Father wants us to do. We are called to walk on water in the midst of the storm, not only after Jesus calms them.

WHAT ARE HIS PLANS AND PURPOSES?

Crossing this ocean of grief and disappointment tried to destroy our family. At times, we felt we were drowning in the endless depths of pain.

On top of that, I was "spitting mad."

For twenty-two years, I prayed the Lord would keep my family—my wife and kids—safe. It was a selfish prayer to keep me from disappointment and pain. When we lost Aly, I was furious with God because He didn't honor what I felt was a negotiated agreement: I sacrifice my life for His kingdom and He protects my family.

From my pain-filled perspective, He didn't keep His side of the agreement, and I was mad about that. However, if I really wanted to go down that road, what I actually negotiated or bargained for, on that day thirty years ago, was a cross. On that cross, I gave my life and all it represents, including my family.

When Michelle and I agreed to follow Jesus, we took up His cross, His suffering, and His sacrifice. The promise was the power of His resurrection! You can't share in His resurrection without sharing in His sufferings and sacrifices. That was the actual bargain.

So, with that "higher" perspective in place, how do we make the transition? How do we get from where we've been to where we need to be? How do we walk on water?

For me, I'm no longer praying for safety to be among my highest desires for my family. Instead, I'm praying they will be drawn into relationship with our Heavenly Father. No matter how long or short their lives may be, my hope and prayer is that, like Aly, they will have an encounter with the Father that radically alters the trajectory of their lives.

This change in perspective only happens when we begin to align our expectations with His plan and purpose. If your expectations are to live a happy life and enjoy the freedoms given you, then you are missing the entire plan of God. If that is your perspective, when a storm threatens to overturn your boat, the last thing you're going to have faith for is walking on water.

He has given us a mandate for our time here on this planet. His mandate is to *"proclaim this message: '*

> *The kingdom of heaven has come near.' Heal the sick, raise the dead, cleanse those who have leprosy, drive out demons. Freely you have received; freely give.'"* (Matthew 10:7-8 NIV)

And:

> *"Go therefore and make disciples of all nations, baptizing them in the name of the Father and of the Son and of the Holy Spirit, teaching them to observe all that I have commanded you. And behold, I am with you always, to the end of the age."* (Matthew 28:19-20 ESV)

This message is not simply for those who have been "called." It's for everyone who has answered "THE call" to be followers of

Jesus Christ. There are no exceptions. It is how we are to live our lives; it is our purpose, our mandate. As followers and Disciples of Christ, we have all been called to walk on water!

> *"Not that I have already obtained this or am already perfect, but I press on to make it my own, because Christ Jesus has made me his own. Brothers, I do not consider that I have made it my own. But one thing I do: forgetting what lies behind and straining forward to what lies ahead, I press on toward the goal for the prize of the upward call of God in Christ Jesus."* (Philippians 3:12-14 ESV)

One of my heroes of the faith is missionary and martyr for Christ, Jim Elliot. I'm on the path I'm on today because of the example of his life recklessly given to the advancement of the Kingdom of God. He had a single focus and a determination to fulfill God's mandate. He gave his life for that cause at an early age.

We refer to him and others like him as "exceptional, unique, and special." He would disagree. He was simply living the life laid out in the Word of God as representing a follower of Jesus. To Jim Elliot, he was living a normal life, not a unique one. He was able to walk that mandate out because he set his expectations on Christ and His upward call.

He shared his perspective on the life of a Christian in a letter to his future wife, Elisabeth Elliot:

"Dearest Betty, 'We are the sheep of His pasture. Enter into His gates with thanksgiving, and into His courts with praise.' And what are the sheep doing going into the gate? What is their purpose inside those courts? To bleat melodies and enjoy the company of the flock? No. Those sheep were destined for the altar. Their pasture feeding had been for one purpose, to test them and fatten them for bloody sacrifice. Give Him thanks, then, that you have been counted worthy of His altars. Enter into the work with praise."[11]

Mark Batterson, lead pastor of National Community Church in Washington, DC, in his book *Not Safe: Discovering God's Dangerous Plan for Your Life,* put it this way:

"Jesus didn't die to keep us safe. He died to make us dangerous. Faithfulness is not holding the fort. It's storming the gates of hell. The will of God is not an insurance plan. It's a daring plan. The complete surrender of your life to the cause of Christ isn't radical. It's normal. It's time to quit living as if the purpose of life is to arrive safely at death."[12]

We are here for a purpose, and it's not to build our careers and our portfolio or to provide a good, safe life for our children so they can simply repeat everything we've done (or not done).

While there is nothing wrong with having a career, being financially stable, and desiring safety for our family, they cannot become our destination or our purpose, or be an obstacle or distraction to it. We're here, for a short period of time, to make a difference, an eternal impact in the kingdom, to be dangerous to the kingdom of darkness, and to train our children to be even more so...another generation that stands on our shoulders because they've watched us give our all for the kingdom. When we begin to reconcile these things to how we live, our expectations fall into alignment with His will.

Over time, disappointments don't carry the weight they once did. We've grown and learned to get out of the boat and to walk on water. Sometimes we look a little like Peter and sink as soon as we take our eyes off of Jesus. What's important though, is we are getting out of the boat, that place of security and comfort, stepping out in faith even though we can't see the bottom.

When we have our eyes set on Him, we adjust our expectations accordingly, and they are no longer based on our circumstances or what we can or cannot do in and of ourselves. Our expectations are squarely placed in His arms. This is where we find the victory in what looked like defeat.

I get it. It seems impossible to find joy and peace in suffering and pain when our expectations and beliefs convince us it's not supposed to be this way.

Don't get me wrong, even when our expectations are set properly and in alignment with Christ, pain is still pain, and it hurts like hell. Being in proper alignment, however, enables us to find the path moving forward—the one that will take us through the shadow of the valley of death and deliver us into the shadow of His wings because we understand His purposes, and that becomes enough.

Did you know?

When we don't understand our purpose, our calling, it makes arriving at the correct destination nearly impossible. The good news is our Heavenly Father has not made it complicated. He has stated His expectations and our mandate very clearly. The problem is we want the journey to be safe and to meet OUR expectations. It doesn't work that way. By becoming His disciples, we have bargained for a cross, so there will be sacrifice along the way. However, you are not alone in your suffering, He is "with you always, to the end of the age."

"The cross is laid on every Christian...When Christ calls a man,
He bids him come and die."
~ Dietrich Bonhoeffer
(German Lutheran pastor, theologian, and anti-Nazi dissident)

Prayer

Dear Heavenly Father,

Forgive me for taking the path that has been more heavily traveled, the path of least resistance. I don't like to suffer, and I don't like the pain associated with it, but I know you gave your life for mine. You took my pain and my suffering, and exchanged it for an eternal relationship with you. I can never repay that gift, but I will give you my life in its entirety right now. Take it. Use it how you see fit, and make me into the child of God you have always intended me to be. Whatever the cost, I am yours. I love you.

In the name of Jesus Christ, amen.

WHO SITS ON THE THRONE?

"I see Christ's love is so kingly, that it will not abide a marrow it must have a throne all alone in the soul."

~ Samuel Rutherford

(Scottish Presbyterian pastor, theologian, and author)

The Lord has been doing a deep work in Michelle and me for many years. It didn't start with the most recent slate of grief and loss. However, He has used this time to take us deeper than we've ever been. That's who He is and that's what He does.

One of those areas He has put His finger on in my life through this season is the reality that my heart has never been His alone. He has always had to share it with other things. And since He doesn't actually share His throne, He's never truly had my heart. For someone who has considered himself a "Christian" for thirty-two years and has been in full-time ministry for more than twenty of those years, that was quite a humbling revelation.

Remember, we're being real here. Aly's death has been a place of discovery for me. It's forced me to face the reality of who is actually sitting on the throne of my heart. Sure, I sing the songs and make the proclamations that He is my king, but then I put other things in His chair. My daughter sat there. She didn't sit there alone. Her siblings, my wife, and the ministry have all had their time in that place, along with countless other things.

Losing Aly has tested every proclamation I've ever made concerning my devotion to the Kingdom of God. We sing songs like "I Surrender All," "Everything and Nothing Else," and Aly's personal favorite, Hillsong's "I Surrender." We make bold statements that God is first in our lives, that He is the center; that does not include my kids, nor does it include Michelle. It is Him and Him alone.

I cannot call myself a follower of Christ if He is not at the center of everything: every thought, every desire, every pursuit, and every decision. It really is ALL or NOTHING—*and I can no longer think those proclamations will not be tested.* Nothing worth its value goes untested. So I have to count the costs of every commitment.

OWNERSHIP

Pain and grief allow us to face some things in our lives. The question is, will we allow the loss and disappointment to push God further from His throne, or will we allow it to tear down the walls so ONLY the King can reside there?

It becomes a question of ownership.

Do other things own and take up the space of my heart or is that set aside and set apart for the King of kings? When my king owns me and has 100% of my heart, I possess everything and NOTHING possesses me.

> *"I have held many things in my hands, and I have lost them all; but whatever I have placed in God's hands, that I still possess."*
>
> ~ Martin Luther

> *"But seek first the kingdom of God and his righteousness, and all these things will be added to you."* (Matthew 6:33 ESV)

"If anyone comes to me and does not hate his own father and mother and wife and children and brothers and sisters, yes, and even his own life, he cannot be my disciple. Whoever does not bear his own cross and come after me cannot be my disciple." (Luke 14:26-27 ESV)

Jesus has never left room for anything but complete abandon to the cause of His kingdom. There are no exceptions.

Unfortunately, we have effectively boiled Christianity down to church on Sunday and a grace message that gives us the freedom to straddle the fence, keeping a foot in each camp while calling ourselves followers of Christ. It doesn't work that way—it never has. If you follow someone, you're doing what they have done and going where they have gone. Period.

HE IS WORTHY OF IT ALL

Michelle and I answered God's call to ministry many years ago as young adults. The call is always the same, "Take up your cross and follow me." When we were young, we didn't understand the fullness of that statement. We didn't understand the sacrifice "taking up your cross" implies.

Of course we considered the material costs…selling our house, furniture, cars, and all our stuff. We knew we would leave our home in the United States and move to another country of vastly different culture and language, and "start all over."

But there were other things we didn't consider—family we would leave behind; parents, grandparents, aunts, uncles, and cousins. The culture we grew up in; the football and baseball games, holiday traditions, school proms, and graduations. These things began to weigh on me as our kids grew up overseas in a Middle Eastern country. We had sacrificed so much, and it didn't register until it was already gone.

I wouldn't have changed it if I could (and my children would all agree because they have loved the life we've lived), but it was still a disappointment for me, a loss of experiences I grew up with. It was my disappointment, not theirs, but it was still a loss I grieved.

It hit especially hard after Aly's death and we had moved back to the states. The school our youngest daughter Annie attends has an end of the year prom. She didn't have a date. She just went for the fellowship and experience, but we still went all out—new dress, manicure, pedicure, wrist corsage, and pictures. We wanted it to be special. As I placed the corsage on her arm, I realized I had never had that experience with Aly, and now she was gone… an opportunity lost forever. The disappointment hit me like a ton of bricks.

I broke down after they left. I completely lost it.

Of course I also cried over the sudden realization my little Annie was no longer so little, and she was growing up fast. Another disappointment.

That was today.

You see, disappointment can find its way into our lives at any point and through any situation. It's a part of life we cannot escape. It feels like a roller coaster most of the time. I've had to learn to roll with it and let it roll over me. I can do that because I know in the end, my Father will have His way, His joy, and His peace. So, I cry. I scream. I even sometimes throw things. I probably need to invest in a punching bag.

Then, I worship. I recommit my life to Him, and I put Him back on the throne of my heart. Why? Because He is worthy of the sacrifice. He is worthy of the pain. Actually, He is just worthy. Period. The more I give to Him, the more I feel a part of His death AND His resurrection; a part of His sacrifice. He really did give everything. I can't even come close to that, so I press on and find He is always faithful.

The bottom line is this: you cannot fully know Christ without knowing the fellowship of His suffering.

Whatever you've gone through or are going through, remember, He is worth the sacrifice. He is worth all of it. So, don't let the enemy steal your sacrifice. It's yours and it is for HIM.

Through it all, remember, He is good. He is faithful.

"I have said these things to you, that in me you may have peace. In the world you will have tribulation. But take heart; I have overcome the world." John 16:33 ESV

That being said, here is His promise. If you will put Him first and place Him and Him alone on the throne, "all these things will be added to you." This is not the idea God is a wishing well or Santa Claus, it's God's promise that everything we need will be provided when we seek Him and His kingdom first.

While that all sounds fine and good, how am I able to reconcile that with the death of my daughter? That's a good question. The truth of the matter is I don't have all the answers, and we'll talk about that in the next chapter. However, I know this...the story is not finished being written for our situation. We don't see the end from the beginning, but He does. I believe Him when He says to keep my focus on Him and His kingdom, and He'll take care of the rest. He is the King, and this is His sovereign territory. When things in my life burn to the ground because I live in a broken world, my Father will make something beautiful out of the ashes. He always has and He always will.

I just need to clear the dust and clutter off of His throne and invite Him, and Him alone, to sit there again.

Did you know?

When God is truly first in your life, everything else that matters is elevated. So, the problems arise when we give His position to other things, even the good things like family, friends, and security. Dying to ourselves and positioning the Lord on the throne of our hearts is a daily exercise, so don't become weary in the sacrifice. Stay the course. Keep Him first.

"There are many who say God is first, yet the words of their mouths have not penetrated the practice of their daily lives."

~ Dr. Mike Hayes

(Author and founding pastor of
Covenant Church, Carrollton, Texas)

Prayer

Dear Heavenly Father,

You have not always been first in my life. Forgive me for putting other things and other people on your throne, for not putting you first in my life. You deserve better. I will do better. Today I proclaim the throne of my heart belongs only to you. These are not just words I am saying, but will be lived out, tested through my actions and the way I live my life. I love you.

In Jesus name I pray, amen.

10

LIVING IN THE MYSTERY

"The ability to embrace mystery is what attracts revelation."

~ *Bill Johnson*

(Best-selling author and Senior Leader,
Bethel Church, Redding, California)

AN UPSIDE DOWN KINGDOM

Obviously, I don't have all the answers. In fact, the more I learn, the more I realize how little I actually know. I find it's one of the things that keeps me pressing into His presence, because only He holds the words of life.

Early in our journey of loss, I was stuck on the "consider it all joy" mandate. I was hurting so much I couldn't even begin to comprehend what James was saying. I must have reread that Scripture passage a hundred times searching for the hidden secrets. How can there be joy in my mourning and peace in my despair? I wanted that, I needed that, but in my pain I couldn't get past the words themselves; they're mutually exclusive, opposites. Yet, if the Word of God says it, I knew, somehow, it must be true, even though it was a mystery. So I pressed in.

The truth of the matter is the Kingdom of God is an "upside down" kingdom. It's backwards to what we consider normal, logical, or acceptable. In fact, God spoke to Isaiah and said:

> *"For my thoughts are not your thoughts,*
> *neither are your ways my ways, declares the LORD.*
> *For as the heavens are higher than the earth,*
> *so are my ways higher than your ways*
> *and my thoughts than your thoughts."* (Isaiah 55:8-9 ESV)

As if to illustrate that passage, Jesus liked to make statements like, *"turn the other cheek," "So the first will be last and the last first,"* and *"Yet it shall not be so among you; but whoever desires to become great among you, let him be your servant."* This is backwards to what society teaches and what culture exemplifies. These are not the statements of a "me" focused culture. We make statements like, "put yourself first because no one else will" and "look out for number one."

Consequently, we don't understand the culture of the Kingdom of God, because it runs counter to the way we've been raised to think of life, society, and freedom. In the culture of the Kingdom of God, Jesus has been anointed...

> *"to grant to those who mourn in Zion—*
> *to give them a beautiful headdress instead of ashes,*
> *the oil of gladness instead of mourning,*
> *the garment of praise instead of a faint spirit;"*
> (Isaiah 61:3a ESV)

SHIFTING THE BLAME

But that doesn't make sense to us, especially in the midst of our pain. Consequently we dismiss much of the Word of God because it doesn't fit in with our way of living life. It doesn't mesh with our cultural and societal norms. So, when faced with disappointment and grief, we become discouraged, confused, and angry. We don't understand. We blame God because we don't really know Him or we have a wrong perception or perspective about Him.

Sometimes we blame the devil because we don't want to wrestle with the thought God was involved; that at some level He had to have "allowed" the circumstance that led to our disappointment and pain. Many times we walk away from God because we don't have answers.

So, we keep blaming Him, the devil, or ourselves, and we look for comfort in other things. The reality is we have to struggle and wrestle with these thoughts and accusations to find His peace. We have to press in deeper to Him and to His presence to find the answers to our pain.

REVELATION IS FOUND IN HIS PRESENCE

There are mysteries in the Kingdom of God we don't understand, and without His revelation, we cannot ever hope to understand them. It only stands to reason that an infinite God would be beyond the understanding of a finite people. Yet, this infinite God wants to be understood. He wants us to wrestle with these issues that have brought us so much pain.

In the story of creation found in the bible, shortly after Adam and Eve had eaten of the forbidden fruit, we read this passage from Genesis 3:8:

"And they heard the sound of the LORD God walking in the garden in the cool of the day, and the man and his wife hid themselves from the presence of the LORD God among the trees of the garden."

I've always found this verse to be comforting, even though it marked the end of their lives in the garden and the beginning of man's toil and pain outside of it.

I find it comforting because of the image of God, the creator of the universe, walking in the garden and enjoying His creation. There is an intimacy being communicated here easily missed by the circumstances Adam and Eve have through their disobedience.

This passage suggests this was a normal occurrence for Adam and Eve and the Lord. The reference to Adam and Eve hiding from His presence indicates they normally wouldn't do that; instead, they would join with Him, in His presence and His walk through the garden.

I sometimes imagine what that must have been like. It wasn't a time of silence and reflection as God, the creator of all things, walked majestically through His creation. I think, in reality, it was a precious and intimate time of wonder, learning, and revelation as the creator, their Father, revealed His creation to the children He entrusted it to. I can imagine the questions Adam and Eve must have asked and the awe His answers must have inspired.

Even though Adam was there from the beginning, it was all a mystery to him, and it was the Father's delight to open up the mystery and begin to reveal its secrets to His creation, His children. I can't fathom what a thrill or how exciting it must have been every day as Adam waited for his creator to "walk through the garden in the cool of the day."

Much of life is learning to live in "the mysteries" of God. It's not always an easy place to be because we constantly want to know "why." We're not satisfied with cliché answers like, "it was just her time to go." We want real answers, but those answers are hard to find. In the process, we have to be willing to live with the mystery while continuing to struggle with those answers that seem out of our grasp.

Here's the "upside down" part again: I think intimacy many times is found in the mystery. The mystery can be something that drives us toward a relationship with the only one who can reveal and unwrap those things we don't understand, like Adam and Eve walking in the garden with God.

"Thus says the LORD who made the earth, the LORD who formed it to establish it—the LORD is his name: Call to me and I will answer you, and will tell you great and hidden things that you have not known." (Jeremiah 33:2-3 ESV)

The phrase "hidden things" is actually one word in Hebrew—basar. It means things inaccessible by fortification. God is saying to Jeremiah, "If you will call to me and seek me, I will answer you and reveal highly fortified things to you that you would NEVER be able to access without me."

It's an invitation to come inside the walls of the castle of the King and be intimate. It implies the creator of the universe wants us to know Him experientially, not just mentally. That's why the answers many times are fortified and impossible to know or understand. He wants us to seek Him. He walks with us, talks with us, leads us and invites us to use our senses and know He is good, that He is for us and has a plan to redeem what has been lost. What an amazingly loving Father we serve.

"Oh, taste and see that the Lord is good! Blessed is the man who takes refuge in him!" (Psalm 34:8 ESV)

I don't want to mislead anyone or for you to misunderstand what has been said. Not everything will be revealed when we want it to be revealed—some things we may never know in this lifetime. But when we accept the invitation to intimacy, then even when we don't understand, when we don't know the "why," we have this promise: *"And the peace of God [that peace which reassures the heart, that peace] which transcends all understanding, [that peace which] stands guard over your hearts and your minds in Christ Jesus [is yours]."* (Philippians 4:7 AMP)

Learning to live in the mystery is paramount to living a life of peace and joy in Christ Jesus. It once again becomes an issue of trust. Trust is not something we usually learn on mountain tops, it's generally what we learn in the valleys—in the dark places and seasons of our lives. It's in the darkness that the light shines its brightest.

Did you know?

If we are seeking answers rather than relationship, both will slip through our fingers. It's intimacy our Father is after, and He will use the mystery to bring us there. He longs for you to walk with Him in the "cool of the day," to seek His face and to know HIM. It's in knowing Him, we find revelation and peace.

> "Because of our selfishness and inclination toward personal comfort and convenience, we'd rather not have to deal with constant change and uncertainty. We have difficulty reconciling the goodness of God with the mystery of his ways."
>
> **~ Chris Hodges**
>
> *(Senior pastor, Church of the Highlands, Alabama)*

Prayer

Dear Heavenly Father,

I don't understand the road I've been on. My lack of understanding has put a wall between you and me. I built that wall. Today, I'm going to take a sledge hammer to that wall because it doesn't belong between us. Teach me your ways and draw me closer to you. I will give you room to be a mystery, while trusting you will reveal those things I need to know...the things that will usher in your presence into my life. I love you.

In the name of Jesus I pray, amen.

LIVING IN THE VALLEY

*"The valley of the shadow of death holds no darkness for
the child of God. There must be light, else there could be no
shadow. Jesus is the light. He has overcome death."*

~ Dwight L. Moody
(American evangelist and publisher)

THIS IS NO TIME TO PANIC

Like many of you, I've walked through a lot of valleys. I tend to
mention the "dark or difficult seasons" in my life in the context
of "being in the valley." That's a fascinating perspective when we
actually think about it.

We typically use the term "valley" to describe all the ugly places in
our lives. We tend to associate it with darkness, pain, and suffering.

Maybe it's because of the familiar passage from David in Psalm 23:4:

> *"Even though I walk through the valley of the shadow of
> death, I will fear no evil, for you are with me; your rod and
> your staff, they comfort me."*

When taken at face value and out of context, this passage can
certainly seem dark and scary. It can make a valley seem like a fearful

place where death and evil lurk behind every bush, boulder, and stone.

In reality, valleys are beautiful places. Those of you who have been in an actual valley (not a metaphorical one), know what I'm talking about. They tend to be rich in vegetation with rivers and wildlife. They are not always dark, and when they are, much of the time it's because of the shadows. When we think about it, eventually, even the mountain tops have periods of darkness. Is darkness really the defining point in our understanding of what is difficult or painful? Darkness only exists where the light is not present. If God is with us, then His light is with us as well.

In Psalm 23 David uses the Hebrew word "yalak" for walk, but it can also mean to be led or carried. That puts a slightly different perspective on it. Being led or carried through the valley adds another dimension to the statement He is with us. He's actually leading and carrying us when we are too shattered to walk. He leads us and carries us *through* the valley; the valley of the shadow of death. Consequently, His light shatters the darkness.

   "Your word is a lamp to my feet and a light to my path."
   Psalm 119:105 ESV

This is also worth saying: God would never lead us or carry us into something evil. It's only when we separate from Him that we become lost in the shadows, where we would otherwise have been guided and directed through them.

Here's something else worth seeing: They are shadows. A shadow is not substantial or permanent; it's momentary, so it doesn't last forever. A shadow can only exist in the presence of light. So where there are shadows, there is a Son. Those places in your life that seem the darkest right now are only shadows, and they are shadows that are cast because of the presence of His light.

I remember when I was sixteen years old, I achieved the rank of

Eagle Scout, the highest honor someone can receive from the Boy Scouts of America (BSA). However, there is an "order" only Eagle Scouts can be a part of. I wanted to be part of it, so I applied. The "test" or "initiation" was spending one night out in the wilderness alone with nothing but a sleeping bag, a canteen of water, two matches, an egg, and a flashlight (I never figured out what I was supposed to do with the egg).

They took me out a few miles in the middle of the Guadalupe Mountains in West Texas in the late afternoon and left me. I had to survive until they came to get me the next morning. Everything was fine until the sun dropped below the backdrop of the surrounding mountains around four o'clock.

From that moment, every sound and the crack of every twig, would catch my breath and cause me to listen intently for anything dangerous. Mountain lions, Bobcats, snakes, scorpions...the area was known for all of them. I was on high alert all through the night. I had thoughts and visions of a mountain lion grabbing me in my sleep. Consequently, I might have slept an hour. I was never more excited than when the sun began to peek over the mountains to the East. The sun was up, the darkness gone, and I had made it. I survived!

When we are in those places, our minds play tricks on us. Are there dangers? Most definitely. Life is full of them, no matter where you're located. But the valleys are no different from the mountain tops. When it's dark, they can both be scary places because our vision is limited. We can't see things well or accurately.

It's in those moments when we begin to see or hear things that aren't there. The perceived isolation brings feelings of fear and paranoia, and our minds tell us things that aren't true. We panic. We run. Then, we get lost.

THINGS GROW IN THE VALLEY

When we walk through disappointment and grief, it sure feels like a dark, damp valley. The world feels like it is closing in on us and we can't breathe. We feel isolated, alone. That's probably similar to what a seed feels like when it's planted in the ground.

> *"Truly, truly, I say to you, unless a grain of wheat falls into the earth and dies, it remains alone; but if it dies, it bears much fruit."* (John 12:24 ESV)

Everyone wants the "mountain top experience" where you're above the clouds in the sun and you can see for miles. It's a great place to be for a moment of clarity and fresh air. The problem is that on the mountain the air is thinner, and it is difficult for things to grow.

Things grow in the valleys.

Yes, for something to grow, something has to die. That's the painful part. That's why it's a valley of death. However, it's also a valley of life. In the valley, death and life coexist in order to create something amazing and beautiful. That's why the valleys are full of trees, fruit, wildlife, and rivers. So, through the death of a single seed (which may bring disappointment and loss), a beautiful forest will grow. The death of one seed produces thousands! That's *life* in the valley of death!

That's why James says to *"Count it all joy, my brothers, when you meet trials of various kinds, for you know that the testing of your faith **produces** steadfastness."* (James 1:2-3 ESV) Our trials in the valley produce fruit in our lives.

There is a dying that must take place in our lives for our Heavenly Father to bring life out of the darkness. We have to let those things die. We have to walk *through* the pain, *through* the valley. Remember, things grow in the valley, so we need to learn to thrive as we walk through them. It's actually a beautiful place to be when we know and understand our creator is with us and is for us, and that He has created the valley as a place for us to grow and learn. Remember, it was in the valley, the garden, that the Father walked with His creation in the cool of the day! It was, and is, a place of discovery and revelation; a place of fellowship and intimacy.

Did you know?

Darkness will lose to the light every time. It's not really even a competition. Try it. Take a light into a dark closet and see what happens. When we are carried or led by the light through the valley, the darkness HAS TO FLEE! We just have to stay the course and follow the light. The valley is not the end of the story, it's just a necessary part of the journey; the part that makes us into the people our Father has always intended us to be.

*"Our faith is built in the dark, in the valleys,
and during the back-breaking battles in life."*

~ Dana Arcuri

(Author, speaker, and certified trauma recovery coach)

Prayer

Dear Heavenly Father,

My life feels dark right now. I am lost in the shadows and can't seem to find you there. I know you are the light of the world. Where you shine, darkness flees. Lead me, direct me, carry me if necessary, but get me THROUGH this valley. Let it do its full and complete work in my life. I want to be complete; I want to be more like Jesus. Have your way in me. I surrender. I love you.

In the name of the only true God, Jesus, amen.

12

THE PLACE OF WORSHIP

If God were small enough to be understood,
He would not be big enough to be worshiped.

~ Evelyn Underhill

(19th century English Anglo-Catholic writer and pacifist)

WHAT WILL YOU WORSHIP?

We were created for worship. That's not an oversimplification, but it's also not complicated, it is *simply* the truth. We WILL worship something. For some, worship might come in the form of a hobby, addiction, or a relationship. Be assured, if we are not intentional in our worship of the One who created us to be worshipers, then our worship will shift to something else. Sometimes it's difficult to recognize, because many of those things may be considered "good" things, like family, ministry, or career.

This goes back to our discussion concerning who sits on the throne. Whoever or whatever has that seat is being worshiped. Sometimes we need to ask ourselves, "Who is on the throne of my heart?"

The issue is there is nothing good apart from God, and when "good" things are worshiped in the place of Him, they become idols, and we will struggle through every disappointment and loss while we worship them.

So, we have to learn to become good at worshiping Him. It must become our first response in every circumstance; the good circumstances and those that seem to wreck our world. It's our only path to recovery.

WORSHIP CHANGES US

Best-selling author and theologian, C.S. Lewis, says: "In the process of being worshiped… God communicates his presence to men."[13]

Worship changes us, and it changes the atmosphere around us. It may not always change the circumstances, but it will certainly change our perspective of them. Perspective matters. It's critical to our ability to make good choices and not quit when things are difficult.

For example, if my perspective is that rainy days are sad and lonely, then, guess what? When it's a rainy day, I will struggle with being sad and lonely. We have to change our perspective, but sometimes that's more difficult than it seems. Consequently, as we discussed earlier, we have to lead ourselves into a new perspective when we recognize our old one is stinky.

Remember my story about returning from the funeral home and making the choice to worship? That decision was made because it wasn't the first time I chose to worship in spite of my circumstances. Over the previous few years, as Michelle and I walked through many disappointments, my experience was that my choice to worship would break the yoke of the enemy over my life. However, I didn't always have that understanding.

I had to break a cycle of self-pity that kept me from truly worshiping the Lord. When things wouldn't go the way I thought they should, when disappointment would set in, I would go to my "pity corner" and pout.

Like we discussed earlier, instead of dwelling in the house of the Lord and changing my perspective, I would choose to dwell on my problems—to camp there. Of course, this only led to resentment, offense, discouragement, and more disappointment. My problems never got better, they only became worse, eventually spreading to my family and other relationships. I was taking a bath in a stinky perspective, and consequently, the atmosphere around my attitude was also stinky.

As I began to discover the impact worship has on my circumstances, I started making the difficult decision to press into His presence, even when everything screamed for me to run to my corner, and my perspective began to change.

THE POSITION OF WORSHIP

I still hear those screams, and I still feel the pull of the enemy to bring me closer. I'm not always perfect in my response, but I fight, and I resist, and I do the things I don't want to do in the heat of the pain. I choose to position myself in a place of worship.

It really is about position.

I played a lot of sports as a young boy and young man. My coaches always taught about "being in position." We often give in to the "head fake" of our opponents. When we do, we find ourselves out of position, and we get beat.

In life, just like sports, we have to know our position. Our position, our posture, is in a place of worship. When we find our circumstances have "head faked" us out of our position, we have to get ourselves repositioned. We have to do what is necessary to find that posture of worship again.

What does that look like for you? Many of you know your position because you've been in it most of your lives. For others, maybe it's not so familiar. For you, there needs to be a season of discovery—a season of positioning yourself in the presence of the King and discovering what that looks like.

It's a daily decision to get in His presence until we discover that place, that position that brings us instantly into His courts and His peace. It's discovered through consistency. Being in His presence must become a priority; making Him first every day.

My position in worship almost always involves music and a place of solitude. I need to be away from other people and distractions where I can put on worship or praise music and turn my attention to Him. I like to write, so I keep a journal of all my thoughts and what I feel the Father is speaking to me in that moment. Some of my most amazing revelations have come in those moments. That's me.

For others, it might be the closet. Maybe it's a walk while you observe the beauty of God's creation. It could be in the morning before everyone else is awake or at night after they've all gone to bed.

Some of my sweetest moments with the Lord have been on long road trips while the family was asleep and it was just me, the road, and my Father.

The how and what are not as important as the "place." I'm not necessarily talking about a physical place, although that might be part of it. In fact, if we are always limiting ourselves to a physical place, then we may struggle to find God when we are somewhere else. Worship is a lifestyle, not an intermission.

The "place" I'm referring to is where you feel free and open to the presence of God without distractions or concerns. It's positioning yourself to meet with the King, your Father. A place or position where everything else fades away and it's just you and Him, the lover of your soul.

The night of the Last Supper, as He was walking with His disciples to the Mount of Olives, Jesus was trying to prepare them for what was about to come concerning His crucifixion.

> *"And when they had sung a hymn, they went out to the Mount of Olives.[31] Then Jesus said to them, 'You will all fall away because of me this night. For it is written, 'I will strike the shepherd, and the sheep of the flock will be scattered.'[32]*

But after I am raised up, I will go before you to Galilee.'"
(Matthew 26:30-32 ESV)

After His death and resurrection, Mary Magdalene, Mary, the mother of James and Salome, went to the tomb to anoint Jesus with oils. Of course, the stone was rolled away, and they were greeted by an angel.

"And he said to them, 'Do not be alarmed. You seek Jesus of Nazareth, who was crucified. He has risen; he is not here. See the place where they laid him.⁷ But go, tell his disciples and Peter that he is going before you to Galilee. There you will see him, just as he told you.'" (Mark 16:6-7 ESV)

Here we have Jesus, before His death and afterwards, telling His disciples He'll meet them in Galilee. Why Galilee? Why not Jerusalem?

That would seem to be the obvious place. It's the place of His death and burial. It's the place of His betrayal, and it's where His followers scattered. I would think He should be there first; walk the streets, let everyone see Him. It would be the ultimate show of victory!

Yet, He goes to Galilee, and it was important enough to Him that He mentioned it before and after His resurrection.

Galilee is a region, not a city. It's a place where Jesus and His disciples spent a lot of time. They took "retreats" there and rested, ministered to one another. I think it's important to note Galilee was home to Jesus and eleven of His twelve disciples (you guessed it, Judas Iscariot, the disciple who betrayed Jesus, was NOT from Galilee).

So, while I would've taken the resurrection to Jerusalem, Jesus took the resurrection home. While I would've wanted to immediately prove to the world they had made a big mistake, Jesus wanted to immediately see His mighty men who were discouraged, disappointed, shattered, and unrecognizable.

He knew this is how they would feel, and He knew they would be broken, that's why He told them beforehand, "I'll meet you at home." He could've met with the world, but He chose to meet with those closest to His heart. He could have met them anywhere, but He chose a place where they had met Him many times, a place that was familiar and significant. It was prearranged. This was their place.

David wrote about this in Psalm 23:

> "The Lord is my shepherd; I shall not want. He makes me
> lie down in green pastures, He leads me beside still waters,
> He restores my soul." (Psalm 23:1-2a ESV)

It's in those places where He leads us that our souls are restored. No matter what we've walked through or the circumstances that surround us on all sides, our Father restores our soul. When we allow Him to position us in places where we can connect with Him, everything else lessens and we become filled with Him and nothing else. Peace. Joy. Restoration.

RETURNING TO THE WELL

When we worship, we place all our issues, concerns, and idols at the feet of Jesus, giving Him full access to His throne in our hearts. It is the ultimate purpose of our lives, and we will find no joy or peace until only He is worshiped there.

It's also not a one-time solution. After Michelle and I returned from the funeral home and I went away to spend time with the Lord and worship, I placed another layer of peace over my grief, but I had to keep going back to the well to receive more and more of that peace. Several months later, I find I must return every day. It really is a journey of worship.

When we choose to take that journey, we find it's not only our best option (as if it's the best of two bad options), but that it's actually an

THE PLACE OF WORSHIP

incredible option—one full of life and adventure, blessing and wonder.

We just have to let Him lead us to that place.

It reminds me of the story of Jesus and the Samaritan woman He met at the well of Jacob. She was a Samaritan AND a woman living in sin. She had obviously seen more than her fair share of pain and disappointment (she had been married five times). Yet, here she stood with the King of kings, the Savior. He offered her a drink from the well, just not the one she had gone to draw from.

> *"Jesus replied, 'If you only knew who I am and the gift that God wants to give you, you'd ask me for a drink, and I would give you living water.' The woman replied, 'But sir, you don't even have a bucket, and the well is very deep. So where do you find this 'living water'? Do you really think that you are greater than our ancestor Jacob who dug this well and drank from it himself, along with his children and livestock?' Jesus answered, 'If you drink from Jacob's well, you'll be thirsty again, but if anyone drinks the living water I give them, they will never be thirsty again. For when you drink the water I give you, it becomes a gushing fountain of the Holy Spirit, flooding you with endless life!'"*
> (John 4:10-14 TPT)

I love how The Passion Translation translates verse 14, "For when you drink the water I give you, it becomes a *gushing fountain of the Holy Spirit, flooding you with endless life!*" This is what happens when we return to the well. It gushes and floods us with His life. If you've ever spent any time in the ocean or in the waves near the beach, you understand the power and force of water. I think that's why Jesus uses this incredible illustration. When we draw from His well, we receive life that can't be stopped. It literally becomes a tidal wave of God's love and passion for us.

When we make worship a daily exercise of positioning ourselves in a place where we can wait on the Lord, we take daily drinks from His well, His Spirit, and it floods us with endless life!

His life. His joy. His peace.

Did you know?

There will be times when it feels like God is a billion miles away. During this season of loss for our family, I have struggled with these feelings. Many times, when we need Him the most, that's when He seems farthest away. If we feel that way, it's always us who have moved. So, in those moments, we need to rediscover our "place" of worship; our Galilee. He's waiting there for us, and He is drawn to the brokenhearted.

"Many a professing Christian is a stumbling-block because his worship is divided. On Sunday he worships God; on weekdays God has little or no place in his thoughts."

~ Dwight L. Moody

Prayer

Dear Heavenly Father,

I can't see you or hear you or feel you. I've moved, but I am coming back to that place of worship right now. I know you are waiting there for me; you've never moved. You've never changed. You've never stopped loving me. I choose you over fear, pain, and disappointment. Help me to rediscover you. I love you.

In Jesus name I pray, amen.

13

PURSUING HIS PRESENCE

"Nothing in or of this world measures up to the simple
pleasure of experiencing the presence of God."

~ A.W. Tozer

DRAWING NEAR

Since we're on the topic and we're being honest, let me just say I've struggled in my relationship with the Lord the past several months.

Before all of this mess began (quarantine, moving back to the United States, and the death of our daughter), I found myself in one of the best places I've ever been. My time with the Lord was sweet and rewarding. My relationships with my wife and kids were better than they had been in a long time. The ministry was growing, and our leadership team was like a family. I felt like I had the bull by the horns and we were on the precipice of something great.

When the news of our daughter's accident came, my world shifted, and everything began to cave in. A chasm developed in my relationship with the Lord, and I couldn't find a way across or around.

I had to force myself to worship or spend any time with Him at all. I just didn't have the energy or the willpower. I was also disillusioned, and my faith was low. Add to all of that the fact I was still angry and you have a perfect recipe for disaster.

Despite all of that, I pressed on. I continued to make time for Him. Truthfully that didn't happen every day. There were days when I was a wreck and couldn't seem to put one foot in front of the other. But I did not give up, and I did my best to stay the course and believe He is who He says He is. Through my doubt, unbelief, pain, anger, and grief, I pressed in. Sometimes because I realized it was my only hope; "all my eggs were in one basket," and I had nowhere else to turn. I was desperate, which doesn't have to be a bad thing. It can be our friend if it drives us into the arms of the only One capable of restoring us.

I still struggle. I'm definitely not back to where I was two years ago, but I'll get there and beyond. Why? Because in His presence there is peace, and in His presence there is joy. In His presence there is strength, forgiveness, and growth. He moves us from glory to glory when we press into Him.

James said it best, *"Draw near to God, and He will draw near to you."* (James 4:8 ESV)

That's just what He does in every situation and in every circumstance...if we will draw near to Him, He is faithful, every time, to draw near to us. The initial movement, however, is up to us. We have to take a step, knowing the most important step we can take is always going to be the next one.

Moses recognized the need for the presence of the Lord. He also knew his people were stiff-necked, stubborn, and disobedient. Consequently, he was concerned they would get to the promised land and the presence of God would not cross over with them. Even after the Lord assured Him that His presence would go with them, Moses wanted to make certain.

"And He said, 'My Presence will go with you, and I will give you rest.' Then he said to Him, 'If Your Presence does not go with us, do not bring us up from here.'" (Exodus 33:14-15 NKJV)

The Lord said, "My Presence will go with you...." Moses was like, "If your presence DOESN'T go with us, WE AIN'T GOIN'!" (Moses was evidently from the Deep South).

Oh Lord, let that be our heart cry in everything we do and in everything we experience (good and bad). If your presence won't be with us, we ain't goin'! No matter what, I will stay in your presence and in the shadow of your wings! *Wherever that may be.*

> *"He gives power to the faint,*
> *and to him who has no might he increases strength.*
> *Even youths shall faint and be weary,*
> *and young men shall fall exhausted;*
> *but they who wait for the LORD shall renew their strength;*
> *they shall mount up with wings like eagles;*
> *they shall run and not be weary;*
> *they shall walk and not faint."*
> (Isaiah 40:29-31 ESV)

HUNGER PAINS

There are not enough words in any language to make you truly hungry for God. To be hungry means you have to go without food for a certain amount of time.

We experience hunger pains when trying to lose weight by sacrificing food for a healthier, lighter body. We cannot expect to be hungry at dinner time if we have just finished stuffing our faces with cake ten minutes before going to the table.

To have a hunger for the Kingdom of God and His presence means we have to deny our spiritual selves from feasting on the junk food this world offers. It starts as a discipline and develops into a lifestyle of hungering after Him.

There is nothing in this book that will do that for you. If you've gathered anything from what we've discussed thus far, I hope you've come to the conclusion that a deep walk in the presence of God comes at a cost. There must be sacrifice. Hunger is developed through trials and tribulations, sacrifice and suffering.

Pursuing the presence of God comes through hungering and thirsting after Him. There is no other angle or shortcut.

> *"As the deer pants for streams of water,*
>   *so my soul pants for you, my God*
> *My soul thirsts for God, for the living God.*
>   *When can I go and meet with God?"* (Psalm 42:1-2 NASB)

For reasons probably best described through expedience, we seem to want a "magic wand" experience with God. We want the hunger, but not the hunger pains. We want to skip over all the things that drive us to the table of fellowship.

There is no magic wand when it comes to a relationship with our Father, unless you want to label sacrifice as the wand. But that's not magic. That's pressing in and trusting Him when everything else is imploding. Sacrifice through trial and disappointment is the only thing that creates a hunger in us so great ONLY the King of kings can satisfy.

THE PURSUIT IN THE WAITING

We also need a better understanding of what it means to be in His presence. We look to things like corporate worship, Bible reading, and prayer as the models for "His presence." Those things are great fire starters or doors into His presence. But, many times the Bible talks about "waiting on the Lord." So often we try to make something happen when our Father simply wants us to remove distractions, clear our thoughts, and wait.

The Lord spoke to Moses and said, *"Come up to me on the mountain and wait there..."* (Exodus 24:12 ESV)

David, multiple times through the Psalms talks of the importance of waiting on the Lord, but I love Psalm 40 from The Passion Translation the best. I think it captures David's amazing heart after God.

> *"I waited and waited and waited some more,*
>> *patiently, knowing God would come through for me.*
>> *Then, at last, he bent down and listened to my cry.*
> *He stooped down to lift me out of danger*
>> *from the desolate pit I was in,*
>> *out of the muddy mess I had fallen into.*
>> *Now he's lifted me up into a firm, secure place*
>> *and steadied me while I walk along his ascending path.*
> *A new song for a new day rises up in me*
>> *every time I think about how he breaks through for me!*
>> *Ecstatic praise pours out of my mouth until*
>> *everyone hears how God has set me free.*
>> *Many will see his miracles;*
>> *they'll stand in awe of God and fall in love with him!"*
> (Psalm 40:1-3 TPT)

The "waiting" David talks about in this passage is not passive, it's active. The actual Hebrew word means to "wait or look eagerly for, to lie in wait for (like a hunter or pursuer)." There is a seeking involved in this type of waiting. It's active, and it's passionate. It's a pursuit.

We can't get where we want to go on our own. There aren't enough books, sermons, songs, or Christian self-help videos to get us there! I heard pastor and international teacher, Paul Manwaring, put it this way (paraphrased), "There's a big difference between 'self-help' and Kingdom…it starts with His presence."

ONLY in His presence is there enough of what we need, and in His presence there is more, more, more…abundantly more than we could ever hope or dream. But we must get better at waiting on Him. In our microwave, fast-food culture, we are in a hurry to see results and find answers, but in God's kingdom, the culture is different. It's a culture of expectancy found in the waiting, in the earnestness of our seeking.

One of my fondest memories of Christmas as a child was not in the presents I received, but in waiting expectantly for something I knew was going to be wonderful—the expectancy that comes with the waiting!

King David is a great role model for our understanding of the presence of God. Being a "man after God's own heart," He literally wrote the book (a good portion of the Psalms) on how to pursue Him.

Psalm 63 is a perfect example of what we are talking about.

He starts the passage off with these very descriptive words:

"O God, you are my God; earnestly I seek you;
  my soul thirsts for you;
my flesh faints for you,
  as in a dry and weary land where there is no water." (ESV)

And then in verse 8 he pens these words:

"My soul follows close behind You;
Your right hand upholds me." (NKJV)

In the English Standard Version (ESV) is translates verse 8 like this:

My soul clings to you....

The word "cling" or "follow" in Hebrew is dabaq. It means to cling or adhere and *to catch by pursuit.*

David paints an amazing picture in this song he wrote for his king, his Lord. He longs for His presence like a man who has been lost in the desert would long for water; when he finds it, he pursues it with everything in him, and when he catches His presence, he clings to it, adhering to it like super glue. He does not let go as his life depends on it. All of this paints an amazing picture of "waiting" and "staying the course," being expectant as we wait on Him.

Our lives depend on His presence.

C. S. Lewis says, "We only learn to behave ourselves in the presence of God."[14]

The message here is one we've been discussing throughout this book; there is movement and action involved in our decision to "follow" Jesus. In other words, it requires pursuit. If you are running after the world, you cannot be running after His presence, the two things are mutually exclusive. "Follower of Jesus" implies pursuit. It implies there is a "chasing" of the presence of God.

It can be no other way.

We've already established that disappointment, suffering, grief, and pain are always going to be a part of life this side of eternity. So, building a foundation of His presence in our lives is critical if we are to find calm in the midst of the storms. If our "pursuit" of His presence only occurs when we are IN the storm, His peace and joy will continue to be elusive and vague, something always just out of reach that we can never quite grasp.

We must establish a lifestyle of pursuing Him. It has to truly become a part of who we are, not a knee-jerk reaction when things fall apart.

THE VEIL IS THIN

Michelle and I recently had breakfast with some very dear friends, Kevin and Melissa Herrin, pastors of The Fellowship Church in Texas City, Texas. While we caught up and discussed the past, present, and future, Kevin spoke an encouraging word to our hearts about our recent loss. He said, and I paraphrase, "Aly is here with us in ways we cannot understand. The veil between this world and the Kingdom of God is so very thin. When we talk about our loved ones being with us, it's more than just the idea that we carry their memory with us wherever we go."

For two days, I couldn't get that thought out of my mind. The reality that the veil between the two kingdoms is thinner than I thought has given more room to the belief I can touch heaven while still on Earth. I have to say, this gives me hope; hope that the reality of eternity is not just a world that exists in some future beyond the grave.

Author and theologian A.W. Tozer writes in his book *The Pursuit of God*, "A spiritual kingdom lies all about us, enclosing us, embracing us, altogether within reach of our inner selves, waiting for us to recognize it. God Himself is here waiting our response to His Presence. This eternal world will come alive to us the moment we begin to reckon upon its reality."[15]

In the midst of all we are going through, God has begun to stir in me a greater desire for more. We live in this world thinking it is the only one that is real and we can't experience heaven until we cross over to eternity. Yet, Jesus tells His disciples to pray, *"Your kingdom come. Your will be done on earth **as it is in heaven**."* (Matthew 6:10 NKJV)

These words from Jesus suggest there is a thinner veil between our two worlds than we are generally willing to believe. It's not just a misty, murky place we can never fully grasp, rather it's more real than anything we've ever experienced on this side of eternity. We can grasp it; reach across the divide and bring heaven to Earth in our lives and in the lives of others. That's actually our mandate. We are ambassadors, this is not our home. Our purpose is to bring the culture of the Kingdom of God to the present culture of man. We are charged to influence and change this culture to His culture.

A.W. Tozer continues, "But we must avoid the common fault of pushing the 'other world' into the future. It is not future, but present. It parallels our familiar physical world, and the doors between the two worlds are open."[16]

The reality of eternity is not just a world that exists in some future beyond the grave, but a place of equal or greater substance than the world on this side. It's separated by a veil so thin it can be experienced in the here and now—a veil hidden by our unbelief and disobedience, fear and selfishness, revealed as we pursue the Father and His kingdom… a Father that is longing to be "caught" and discovered.

This is an important concept to grasp as we struggle with disappointment, grief, or anything else that might have turned our story upside down. His presence is available. Heaven is not so far away. The doors of fellowship have been flung wide open, and He is closer than you think.

A.W. Tozer continues, "If we would rise into that region of light and power plainly beckoning us through the Scriptures of truth we must break the evil habit of ignoring the spiritual. We must shift our interest from the seen to the unseen. For the great unseen Reality is God. 'He that cometh to God must believe that he is, and that he is a rewarder of them that diligently seek him.' This is basic in the life of faith. From there we can rise to unlimited heights."[17]

"From the moment John stepped onto the scene until now, the realm of heaven's kingdom is bursting forth, and passionate people have taken hold of its power." (Matthew 11:12 TPT)

There is more; so much more for us to experience. Are we content to stay in our places of comfort, arriving safely at the grave, or are we willing to reach out and grasp His kingdom now? The pursuit of His presence requires taking risks and doing things that are uncomfortable. What are you going to pursue?

Did you know?

As we begin to understand that His kingdom, His presence, is not only available, but waiting for our discovery, we will find it is the only place of true peace in this lifetime. Everything else, the things of this world, will provide nothing more than a temporary solution. He is the only way, He is the only truth, and He is the only life. No one finds peace except that it comes through Him.

"Our pursuit of God is successful just because He is forever seeking to manifest Himself to us."

~ A.W. Tozer

Prayer

Dear Heavenly Father,

I feel lost without you. I miss you. I miss talking with you and hearing your voice. I need you more now than ever. I will take time, this very moment, to wait on you. I am yours. I lay my time down, my anxiety down, and my doubt. I will move when you move. I'm told the veil is thin, so open up the heavens and reveal yourself to me in a way I have never experienced. I love you.

In beautiful name of Jesus I pray, amen.

THE TABLE OF INTIMACY

"Royalty is my identity. Servanthood is my assignment.
Intimacy with God is my life source."

~ Bill Johnson

AN INVITATION

In my Bible studies over the past several months, I haven't been able to move past John 13 and 14. I've been greatly impacted by the last days of Jesus and His response of love and intimacy toward His disciples. From John leaning on Jesus during the Last Supper to Jesus washing the feet of His disciples, "He loved them to the end." (John 13:1b ESV)

I'm convinced our salvation journey is directly linked to our response of love and intimacy with our Heavenly Father; not simply to words spoken in a prayer in a moment of influence. The phrases "Depart from Me for I never *knew* you," and "Well done good and faithful servant" are defining phrases of intimacy and invitation. It's not an invitation to heaven, although that is part of the "package," but an invitation to draw near and lean on the Savior, the King, our Father, our friend.

The prayer we pray means nothing if not followed by a focused pursuit of intimacy. We rarely, if ever, read of Jesus speaking of

His love, rather it's expressed in the very fabric of His actions and the way He lived life. Consequently, it's not so much about what we say as much as it is who we become. In other words, it's not the journey or destination that matters as much as how we arrive there. Of course, how we arrive depends greatly on how we mature during the journey.

Referring back to Psalm 23, one of my favorite verses in this chapter comes after verse 4, *"Though I walk through the valley of the shadow of death, I will fear no evil, for you are with me; your rod and your staff, they comfort me."* Then, in verse 5, David writes this, *"You prepare a table for me in the presence of my enemies."*

A TABLE OF INTIMACY

Having spent sixteen years living in the Middle East, I have a unique view on this verse. In the West, pursuit of our careers, wealth, happiness, and other things have slowly eroded the intimacy of the family. Please don't misunderstand that statement. I didn't say it eroded the "love" of the family (although that is the next thing to go), but rather the intimacy. They're different, but we sometimes make them to be the same thing. We can love someone and not have a close relationship with them, not really "knowing" them.

I had an interesting conversation with a Muslim at a conference years ago. After discussing the virtues of Christianity versus Islam, he made this statement: "In Islam we believe Jesus and we believe He come to earth again one day. He is not the Son of God or God. But, I love Jesus like crazy!" While this may produce a little smile or giggle (I tried to capture the accent and grammar), I believe he was truthfully saying he loved Jesus. However, he didn't know Him. Until he does, eternity will remain just out of his grasp.

Despite this and other shortcomings, I have found that in the East, family is first. It's not perfect by any stretch of the imagination, but there is intimacy. Much of that intimacy happens around food and drink. In many parts of Central Asia and the Middle East, there is still no "table." A tablecloth is spread out on the floor, and the food is served there while the family leans against each other and serves one another. They tell their stories of the day and laugh, argue, and cry together. It's intimate. It's close. It's family.

So, when David writes, *"You prepare a table for me in the presence of my enemies...,"* there is an entire cultural context behind it. It's not a reference to a simple meal prepared by a loving Father. It tells a story of a place of family, a place of peace; it's a safe place, a place of intimacy. I recently hear Bill Johnson calls it a "table of intimacy."

It's at this table where fellowship happens. It's at this table where problems are discussed and hope is encouraged. It's at this table where our identity is established as children of the King. It's at this table where we find the enemy has no hold on us.

In the presence of our enemies (fear, shame, guilt, offense, discouragement, depression, and too many others to list), He prepares a table of intimacy and commands the enemy to stop, to desist, to stand back. It's the ultimate humiliation. It says to your enemies, I am not concerned with you or intimidated by your little battle. I only care about my child and his growth, character, and relationship with Me. Our Father desires intimacy.

This is what happens during the darkest moments in our lives when we allow the Lord, our heavenly Father, to set up His throne in our hearts. Nothing can overcome intimacy with Him. He rules the day, and He is in control of the battle.

Did you know?

When a table is prepared "in the presence of our enemies," it is assumed in that moment, there is peace. It's when we follow Him through the valley that He brings peace through intimacy. You see, it's not just about being led or carried through the valley, but it's about how we relate to our Father. We must intentionally pursue Him.

If experiencing the valley, don't allow the darkness, the shadows to pull you away. He has something amazing prepared for you, but you must accept the invitation and take your place at the table.

"The Spirit of God is jealous over us; He doesn't want superficial fellowship, but genuine intimacy."

~ John Bevere

(International minister and best-selling author)

Prayer

Dear Heavenly Father,

I am constantly amazed at your pursuit of my heart. Forgive me for the times I've taken that for granted. Help me to better understand your love for me. I give you my heart and I accept your invitation of intimacy. I will pursue you in spite of the difficulties I'm walking through right now. I will follow you through the valley and take a seat at your table. I love you.

In the precious and holy name of Jesus, amen.

15

THERE IS HOPE IN THE PAIN

"We are not necessarily doubting that God will do the best for us; we are wondering how painful the best will turn out to be."

~ C.S. Lewis

REWARDING FAILURE

I don't like pain. My wife will tell you I have a low tolerance for it (remember my story about back pain). I'm the guy who can't watch the doctor give his kids shots. I don't like receiving pain, and I don't like giving it. Being a parent and in full-time ministry for more than twenty years, that's been a challenge for me, because, even though it's cliché, if there's no pain, there's no gain. That's an old physical fitness idiom, but it applies to our spiritual and emotional fitness as well.

I read this poem from an unknown author, and it resonated with me:

"Sometimes you must hurt in order to know, fail in order to grow, lose in order to gain, because most of life's greatest lessons are learned through pain."

Simply put, you can't grow into the man or woman God has purposed you to be without pain. The same applies to those you lead or train. You can't raise children or leaders without allowing them to fail. Failure and pain are a critical part of the process.

That's why the valleys are so important.

Knowing that, we should be better at rewarding failure. When we can get good at failing, then taking risks won't seem so scary and painful. Taking risks is necessary because it puts our faith in the ONLY One who can do anything great. It says, "This is too big for me...only God can do it, so, I'm going to see what He will do."

Our Father is good. He is not intimidated by our failure, rather, He's ACTIVATED by our willingness to take a risk, especially when failure may seem imminent.

Two of my favorite Bible characters are Caleb and Jonathan. I like them because, for me, they represent total faith in God. They were risk takers. Some might even say foolhardy. Let's look at a couple of their more famous stories.

In Joshua 14 we see the Israelites have finally made it into the promised land and they are assigning the parcels of land according to the tribes of Israel. Caleb was eighty-five years old, and he approached Joshua and makes a bold request.

> *"As yet I am as strong this day as on the day that Moses sent me; just as my strength was then, so now is my strength for war, both for going out and for coming in. Now therefore, give me this mountain of which the LORD spoke in that day; for you heard in that day how the Anakim were there, and that the cities were great and fortified. It may be that the LORD will be with me, and I shall be able to drive them out as the LORD said."* (Joshua 14:11-12 NKJV)

In a manner of speaking, he says, "Don't give me the easy, low hanging fruit. I'll take the mountains. You know, the ones where the giants are still living." And then he says these words, *"It may be that the LORD will be with me...."* His choice of words indicated Caleb wasn't 100% certain of the outcome; he was taking a risk.

He was trusting in the Word of the Lord over his life and stepping out to do something crazy and potentially costly. He knew his God, his Father, and he knew He was good! So, he put God on the spot. I LOVE IT!

Approximately 400 years later there was another story involving King Saul's son and King David's best friend, Jonathan. The enemy of the Israelites, the Philistines, were encamped against them. The Israelites had no weapons. Only Saul and his son, Jonathan, had any. So, they were all just sitting around. Jonathan, I believe, was probably not great at "waiting around," and he got tired of sitting and decided to do something about it.

> *"Then Jonathan said to the young man who bore his armor, 'Come, let us go over to the garrison of these uncircumcised; it may be that the LORD will work for us. For nothing restrains the LORD from saving by many or by few.'"* (I Samuel 14:6 NKJV)

Do you see the language? It's exactly what Caleb said 400 years earlier, *"It may be that the LORD will work for us."*

IT MAY BE? He was risking his life and that of his armor bearer on a maybe— dangerous words and possibly the worst military strategy in the history of military strategies.

I can only imagine what his armor bearer thought, "Why do I follow this guy around? One of these days Jonathan is going to get me killed!" But to his credit, he got in alignment with his leader. He was probably accustomed to his boss taking crazy risks. I can't imagine this story is Jonathan's only foray into the extreme and dangerous. Like his best friend David, he was used to putting God's promises to the test.

What was the conclusion of the story? Jonathan and his armor bearer killed twenty men within a half-acre of land, and then God got involved:

"That first slaughter which Jonathan and his armor bearer made was about twenty men within about half an acre of land. [15] And there was trembling in the camp, in the field, and among all the people. The garrison and the raiders also trembled; and the earth quaked, so that it was a very great trembling. [16] Now the watchmen of Saul in Gibeah of Benjamin looked, and there was the multitude, melting away; and they went here and there." (1 Samuel 14:14-15 NKJV)

That's what happens when we allow God to build in us character and faith through trials, suffering, and failures. We begin to take risks we would never have taken. We are no longer afraid of failure or the pain it brings. We don't fear persecution or suffering because we have seen the grace, mercy, and power of the Lord firsthand! We have lived it. We have grown through it. We are better and stronger for it.

It's in those times our heavenly Father can come in and begin to do a work in us that strengthens our spiritual and emotional "muscles." We get stronger through the trials and the pain. We're able to carry more weight. We become better people with stronger character and a more focused sense of purpose. We find the passion that burns so hot for our Savior, and then we become fire starters, through our lives sparking the flames in others.

Or, we can be like those people who have great intentions for their New Year's resolutions, and then, after the first week in the gym, they quit, because it was too painful. They never make it to that place where strength is developed and they can run further and lift more. They stay unhappy with their weight, sluggish in life, and unable to reach their potential because they constantly run from pain. I've been there, I'm sure you have, too. However, pain is not only a part of life, it's a necessity! It's the only path to growth.

In this season of recovery, Michelle and I have made a commitment to get in better shape physically. We have come to realize our lives are but a breath and we will never reach our full potential if we are not at our best physically, emotionally, spiritually, and mentally. We're in it for the long haul. It's a marathon, not a sprint. So we've made some changes to our diet and our conditioning.

The first month was hard. I dreaded "workout days." I was out of shape and it showed. As I pressed in however, I began to appreciate the pain and soreness I had the next day. When I didn't have it, I knew there was no new muscle growth. I began to miss it. Now, several months in, I'm stronger, I feel better, think more clearly, and sleep better at night. Pain brought me to this point, and pain will take me further.

It wasn't easy, and certainly not always enjoyable, but I'm no longer afraid of it. I know now that when pain is present, I'm growing and I'm healing. It's a sign I'm alive and He is working in me, strengthening me, restoring me, and preparing me for the work of the kingdom.

DELAYED HEALING

Strengthening and healing takes time, and of course it's different for everyone. Much of our response and the way we handle disappointment depends on a lot of factors; personality, past experiences and hurts, family and friends, age…the list goes on and on. For some, it seems they can recover and find their footing sooner than others. For most, the recovery seems to take forever.

Today was a perfect example. This week marks ten months since our daughter passed away. The day started great. It's Saturday, our "chore day." We all have a list of what needs to be done to clean the house. We each have responsibilities.

Our youngest son, age twelve, started off great. He was half done with his chores before breakfast was ready. While finishing breakfast (Michelle was gone for the day attending a conference), I casually mentioned a few other things that needed to be done. When I mentioned vacuuming the family room, there was an argument over who was going to do it. Our son fell apart and went to his room furious. That's not like him, but it was becoming a pattern.

When I went upstairs to talk with him about it, he started crying. His face went from expressions of extreme frustration to sadness. I moved over next to him, recognizing there was more going on here, and said to him, "You loved her, it's okay to be sad." He completely lost it and said he misses her. It was one of the few times in ten months he has even been willing to talk to us about the loss of his older sister. He cried into my chest for about twenty minutes. I just let him cry. Breakthrough. Ten months later.

Timing is important, and it's even more important we don't rush what God is doing. Oh, we need to be proactive, pursuing Him and healing, but we can't put a time frame on pain, grief, or disappointment.

After about six months from Aly's death, I began to feel pressure (from myself more than others) to "get over it" as if there was some magical date that grace for such things expires. Yet, I felt I should be stronger than this, or others would think I seem stuck in my grief. Everyone approaches disappointment differently, and it takes some people longer to find their footing than others. And that's okay.

We have to give ourselves (and others) room, and the grace that goes with it, to get through. We must go through; not over or around, but through. Sometimes it feels like running the gauntlet.

We get beat up and beat down along the journey, but when we stay the course and allow the journey to have its full effect on our lives, we arrive at our destination better than when we started, albeit different.

Disappointment and grief changes us—that's just the plain truth, and there is no way to avoid it. If we will let it, however, it will change us into something amazing; something closer to His image. But it takes time.

Did you know?

Failure, pain, disappointment, and loss are not the end of the journey. Many times they are simply the beginning of a new one. It can be a journey that takes you to surprising and exciting destinations if you let it. More than anything, however, they are the stepping stones to becoming something better, something stronger, something more like Jesus; but there will be pain. Pain is very much a part of the process, it's actually necessary for proper growth and maturity. If we can learn to embrace the pain and let it do its work in us, we will find hope in it.

"The little troubles and worries of life may be as stumbling blocks in our way, or we may make them stepping-stones to a nobler character and to Heaven. Troubles are often the tools by which God fashions us for better things."

~ Henry Ward Beecher

Prayer

Dear Heavenly Father,

I have fallen and I have failed in this journey. Thank you for being there to help me pick up the pieces. Take them and build something better, stronger, and more like you. Build something that will stand when the struggles and storms of life come. Build something that will draw the brokenhearted and beaten down. Let me be a building others will be able to run into. Make me like you. I love you.

In Jesus name I pray, amen.

16

THERE WILL BE SCARS

"The sudden disappointment of a hope leaves a scar which the ultimate fulfillment of that hope never entirely removes."

~ Thomas Hardy
(English novelist and poet)

WOUNDS THAT HEAL

Many times, when we've experience trauma or pain of some kind, we're left with scars. We all have them. Scars are generally things we cover up because we think they are ugly, and also because, many times, they are reminders of the trauma that caused them.

I've got several scars. Some of them I'm proud of, like the one I have just above my right eye from when I fell off my bike when I was eight. I set up a ramp trying to jump the curb with my bicycle and missed—a moment I took great pride in when telling my friends. Some of my scars are embarrassing like the one on my left arm where I cut myself painting...yes, painting. Through 2020, my cache of scars has grown.

The problem for most of us is we want our healing to include the scars. We don't want a remembrance of the pain. We just want to erase it from existence and pretend it never happened. We tend to forget a scar is no longer a wound, but rather a sign the wound has healed. There may be some phantom pains or some scar tissue that flares up from time to time, but for the most part, the painful time that comes with the healing process has passed.

So, why is it we still tend to find them so unpleasant? Why do we cover them and hide them from others? It's usually because they are painful and ugly reminders of where we've been. If we've never dealt with the pain, if we've gone around it or over it, never through it, then we're really not looking at a scar, we're actually still dealing with an open wound we're calling a scar. Open wounds are definitely ugly. There hasn't been proper healing or growth, and they become infected and ooze nasty, green puss.

However, properly cared for, wounds will heal. And after they heal, many become scars, which become identifiers of how far we've traveled, the destinations we've reached; the chances and risks we've taken, the failures we've overcome.

Christian evangelist, songwriter, and author, Sheila Walsh, says it best, "Scars are proof that God heals."[18] If you've been through loss, grief, disappointment, and pain, (that would be everyone) then you have scars. Don't cover them up. Let people see that you bear the emblem of pain, you walk in healing, because Jesus still heals.

JESUS HAS SCARS

The truth of the matter is Jesus has scars. You would think after the resurrection He would be new and completely restored. But, He still carried His scars. I heard a sermon many years ago from the founding pastor of Covenant Church in Carrolton, Texas, Mike Hayes. I believe the title was "He Still Bears Our Scars." In the sermon he talked about what the resurrected Jesus looked like. Why didn't His closest friends immediately recognize Him?

It all begins in John 20:14 with Mary Magdalene,

"Now when she had said this, she turned around and saw Jesus standing there, and did not know that it was Jesus."

This is the woman who anointed Jesus' feet with expensive perfume and then cleaned them with her hair as an act of sacrifice and humility. Yet, she didn't immediately recognize Him after His resurrection.

Then, in John 20:19-20 (NKJV) Jesus is with His disciples,

"Then, the same day at evening, being the first day of the week, when the doors were shut where the disciples were assembled, for fear of the Jews, Jesus came and stood in the midst, and said to them, 'Peace be with you.' When He had said this, He showed them His hands and His side. Then the disciples were glad when they saw the Lord."

After He showed them His scars, *then* they recognized Him. Eight days later, they are gathering again and Thomas is there:

"And after eight days His disciples were again inside, and Thomas with them. Jesus came, the doors being shut, and stood in the midst, and said, 'Peace to you!' Then He said to Thomas, 'Reach your finger here, and look at My hands; and reach your hand here, and put it into My side. Do not be unbelieving, but believing.' And Thomas answered and said to Him, 'My Lord and my God!'" (John 20:26-28 NKJV)

Let me give you the simple truth as to why Jesus' closest friends didn't recognize Him; it's because He was unrecognizable.

"Just as many were astonished at you, so <u>His visage was marred</u> more than any man, and His form more than the sons of men;" (Isaiah 52:14 NKJV)

"And I looked, and behold, in the midst of the throne and of the four living creatures, and in the midst of the elders, stood a Lamb <u>as though it had been slain</u>..." (Revelation 5:6 NKJV)

Here was a man who endured the most horrific and terrible torture any man has ever had to endure. Isaiah says He was so beaten He wasn't recognizable. Even in heaven, John said the Lamb (Jesus) looked as though He had been slain.

The resurrection did not remove Jesus' scars. We know He carries the scars to His hands, His feet, and His side because He showed them to Thomas and the others.

I don't know what your mental picture is of Jesus after the resurrection, but in spite of the scars, it's important we understand He is our conquering hero—He won't return on a lowly donkey—He will return in authority on a white war horse. Yet, He bears battle scars, badges of courage. He healed everyone He touched, but He chose not to cover up His own scars. He healed the ten lepers, He restored their missing fingers and ears. Their skin was perfect and new, but He left His scars.

Why would He leave them there? Listen to the words of the Prophet Zechariah.

"⁶ And one will say to him, 'What are these wounds between your arms?' Then he will answer, 'Those with which I was wounded in the house of my friends.'" (Zechariah 13:6 NKJV)

His scars say two things:

"I was here before and you didn't know me." His scars are evidence He is not the "new" Messiah, but He was here before—He's the "returned" Messiah.

It also says He's not a Savior untouched by our needs. He bore our sin, sickness, and shame. "He's been tempted in every way we are, yet He has overcome!"

He bears the marks in His body of His visit to this world where He suffered and was tempted in every way. It says He can identify with our pain.

Your scars do the same. They bear the mark of your visit to this world and the testimony of your healing. God will use your scars to help others who are still in that place of pain from the wound. Your scars tell them you've been where they are, you can identify with their pain, and you have overcome!

But, you have to let people see them. You cannot be ashamed of where you've been and what you've walked through. You are victorious in Christ. Let your place of wounding become a testimony of God's resurrection power, but carry the scars so everyone knows who you are and where you come from. They are not ugly. They are the sign He has taken your ashes and made them beautiful.

Did you know?

Michelle and I carry scars. Throughout our journey, we've made the decision to keep our scars uncovered. We've made the decision to invite others into our pain and our disappointment. In doing that, we've also given them a front row seat to God's grace and His victory over grief. You can't let people see one without the other. Scars. They can be a testimony to the world of God's faithfulness, goodness, and love. Show them off.

"Scars are our reminder that we can get up and walk again."

~ Kelly Balarie

(Author and blogger)

Prayer

Dear Heavenly Father,

I have scars. Of course, you know that. You know each one, and you know the details of every story behind every scar. To you, they are beautiful. They are the symbols of my journey with you and the times I stumbled, tripped, and fell; yet continued and did not quit. You are proud of those scars because they show you had the final say. Thank you for my scars. Thank you that for each and every time I fell down, you were there to pick me up, dust me off, and lead me through the pain. I love you.

In the name of the only One who holds my heart, amen.

BROKENNESS AND VULNERABILITY

*"We will never meet God in revival until
we have first met Him in brokenness."*

~ Nancy Leigh DeMoss
(Christian author and radio host)

A COMPASSIONATE SAVIOR

*"The LORD is near to the brokenhearted
    and saves the crushed in spirit.
Many are the afflictions of the righteous,
    but the LORD delivers him out of them all."*
(Psalm 34:18-19 ESV)

Any conversation about brokenness must begin with Psalm 34. David was clearly a man and a leader who understood what it meant to be broken, through his own poor choices and the choices of others. He also knew how close the Father is to the brokenhearted. Many of the Psalms were written from his multitude of disappointments.

Our brokenness, pain, and disappointment is like a beacon to the compassion of Christ. He comes running toward those who are vulnerable and crushed.

In fact, in describing His purpose and mission on earth, Jesus read from Isaiah these words:

> *"The Spirit of the LORD is upon Me,*
> *Because He has anointed Me*
> *To preach the gospel to the poor;*
> *He has sent Me to heal the brokenhearted,*
> *To proclaim liberty to the captives*
> *And recovery of sight to the blind,*
> *To set at liberty those who are oppressed;*
> *To proclaim the acceptable year of the LORD."*
> (Luke 4:18-19 NKJV)

If you're broken and hurting, believe it or not, you're in a good place. So often, in our pain and disappointment, we want to hide and pretend we are okay. We don't want anyone to see our wounds and the scars they leave behind. Consequently, we hide from the very one who can lead us through the pain.

VULNERABILITY ACTIVATES HIS HEALING

Vulnerability, on the other hand, gives life to humility and shatters pride. It allows the Holy Spirit to be activated over our pain. When we are open about our brokenness, the Spirit of God is released to fulfill His purpose; to heal and set us free.

David uses the Psalms to express his brokenness, as well as his victories. In the Psalm 31 we see a perfect example of David's vulnerability as he cries out to his Heavenly Father:

> *"Have mercy on me, O LORD, for I am in trouble;*
> *My eye wastes away with grief,*
> *Yes, my soul and my body!*
> *For my life is spent with grief,*

And my years with sighing;
My strength fails because of my iniquity,
And my bones waste away.
I am a reproach among all my enemies,
But especially among my neighbors,
And am repulsive to my acquaintances;
Those who see me outside flee from me.
I am forgotten like a dead man, out of mind;
I am like a broken vessel."
(Psalm 31:9-12 NKJV)

Whatever you may think of David, he was a vulnerable king. He lays it all out before the Lord, holding nothing back. He lists not just his pain, but how crushed he feels in spirit. This is what the Lord longs for in us—a rawness, an intimacy not hindered by the walls we've constructed to make us look stronger than we are. He's not intimidated by your pain or my pain. Rather, He's drawn to our weaknesses. He's activated by our honesty and humility. Remember, it's in our weakness He is strong.

It's critical we talk about brokenness. We live in a church culture (and world culture) that teaches us to hide our weaknesses and struggles; to "pull ourselves up by our own bootstraps" so to speak (an impossibility I might add; I've tried).

If you are a pastor, church leader, or in ministry of some kind, it can be especially difficult as we tend to feel we've been put on a pedestal, either voluntarily or involuntarily. There is the false perception that because we are in ministry, we should be better and more "righteous" than those who are not. Once we allow ourselves to be exalted to that level, it's easy to be knocked off. The fall is usually tragic and painful. The only solution to the "pedestal problem" is transparency. Whether your leadership is through the church, the family, or community, we stay on equal footing by being open about our failures and shortcomings.

If we examine the Scriptures, we see our Heavenly Father is drawn to our pain, oppression, and disappointment. Knowing that, why would we want to hide them? I guess it's a similar situation to Adam and Eve in the Garden of Eden as they hid from the Lord. They knew they were naked, so they were ashamed. They didn't realize He already knew their situation, He just wanted them to come clean, be vulnerable, and throw themselves into His arms. Instead, they made excuses, pointed fingers, and continued to hide their fear and hurt.

I sometimes wonder what would've happened if they had just run to Him, confessed what they had done, asked His forgiveness, and allowed Him to minister to their brokenness. I don't really wonder. I know my Father. He would've healed them and restored them, because "He is near to the brokenhearted."

A BROKEN BRIDGE

There is a second benefit to our vulnerability and brokenness. Sheila Walsh says, "My brokenness is a better bridge for people than my pretend wholeness ever was."[19] Christian singer-songwriter Jason Gray says, "When I come clean about my brokenness, others catch glimpses of how the real grace of a real God works in the messy life of a real person."[20]

I love that. Our brokenness, our messy lives, can be a bridge for others to find healing in Jesus. Upside down (or catawampus as we say in the South). Consequently, we struggle to understand how our broken lives can be a blessing to someone else. My life is a mess. It's shattered, unrecognizable. How can it be used to bring wholeness to others?

As Jesus said in Revelation 21:5, "Behold, I make all things new." Your life may be shattered and unrecognizable, but it will be something new and wonderful when you are vulnerable and allow the Father to be the Father. When people see your scars and hear about your journey through disappointment, they will also see God's hand of deliverance, and it will give them hope in their situation.

It will also show them there is a path through the valley and a Savior walking it with them.

Did you know?

Vulnerability in our brokenness brings healing. I know, it sounds backwards, but it works. In our honesty, humility, and transparency, God brings His healing. He's drawn to it. There is something about being laid out in total surrender that our Heavenly Father cannot turn His back to. In fact, He runs to the vulnerable and brokenhearted. That's just who He is and how deeply He loves us.

> "God uses broken things. It takes broken soil to produce a crop, broken clouds to give rain, broken grain to give bread, broken bread to give strength. It is the broken alabaster box that gives forth perfume. It is Peter, weeping bitterly, who returns to greater power than ever."
> **~ Vance Havner**
> *(Revivalist and author)*

Prayer

Dear Heavenly Father,

I am broken beyond recognition. This really hurts and I want it to stop. But, I want the pain and the brokenness to have its complete work in me. I give you permission to pick up the pieces of my broken life and make it into whatever you want. I am yours. I surrender and I love you.

In your Son's name I pray, amen.

18

THE PARADOX OF PEACE

"Life with God is not immunity from difficulties,
but peace in difficulties."

~ C.S. Lewis

RELEASING FEAR

Fear. How will I pay the rent this month? What if I don't get the job? What if I try and fail? What will people think? I have to keep my children close and protect them because they might get hurt.

There are other types of fear as well. As a child, I remember always wanting the hall light on so my room wasn't too dark. "Mom, could you check the closet and under my bed?"

Fear is what keeps us from becoming everything God has purposed us to be. It's what keeps us from taking risks. Fear actually paralyzes us and keeps us from stepping out; trembling while we hide under the covers and hope if we are still and quiet it will go away. "Oh, that's too dangerous" or "I could never afford to do that." We have so many fears in our lives. Fear of the unknown. Fear of failure. Fear of the dark. The technical term is "phobia."

Agoraphobia-Fear of being in crowds, public places, or open areas

Acrophobia-Fear of heights

Claustrophobia-Fear of confined spaces

Arachnophobia-Fear of spiders (Okay, this one might be legitimate)

Anglophobia-Fear of England or English culture

(Okay, I threw that last one in for giggles and to give all my British friends a chuckle.)

The fact is, there is a phobia for just about everything. I don't have enough time or pages to list them all.

Our Father never intended for us to walk in fear. In fact, His message to Adam was to "fill the earth and subdue it and have dominion" over it. God intended us to walk in His authority and in His peace. Fear was never to be part of the equation. The enemy brought that when He was able to separate man from His purpose and His creator. He's still doing that today even though we walk under the same mandate as Adam and Eve.

> *"For you did not receive the spirit of bondage again to fear, but you received the Spirit of adoption by whom we cry out, 'Abba, Father.'"* (Romans 8:15 NKJV)

> *"For God has not given us a spirit of fear, but of power and of love and of a sound mind."* (2 Timothy 1:7 NKJV)

Notice the wording in these two verses. Paul uses the word "again" in his letter to the Romans referencing our bondage to fear due to Adam's choices. The inference here is Jesus' sacrifice restored us to our original design. It's a warning not to allow the enemy to once again pull us away from our mandate. We are called to subdue and have dominion.

To Timothy, Paul uses another word important to see—power. God didn't give us a spirit of fear, but power. Authority. Dominion.

The enemy hates our position of authority. He wants to take it from us.

"The thief comes only to steal and kill and destroy. I came that they may have life and have it abundantly."
(John 10:10 ESV)

Fear is a thief. It will attempt to steal, kill, and destroy our peace. However, in truth, fear is not strong enough unless we give it authority in our lives. Jesus' sacrifice and resurrection gave us victory over fear. Now, we have abundant life. It's guaranteed to us because of His sacrifice, but we have to choose it every day, because the enemy will not relent. He has a goal, and at its core is fear. He will use every circumstance to pull us away from our identity as children of the Most High King.

The victory, and the reminder, is our Heavenly Father will use every circumstance to usher us into His peace and purpose if we will choose Him.

A MESSAGE OF PEACE

In December of 2020, just five months after Aly passed away, Michelle wrote this incredible Facebook post about peace I wanted to share. I feel it encapsulates exactly what we've been discussing throughout this book:

2020, for many, maybe even most, has been a difficult year. A year of unexpected pain, loss, confusion. Maybe you have lost hope. Maybe your faith has been stretched, challenged, tested and unbelief exposed. Mine has been, I'll be honest. Some of you, knowing the pain, or some of it, that we have lived through this year, may say, "Well, that's to be expected or understood." During this "Advent" season and the coming of a new year, we use words and talk about the ideas of love, hope, joy and peace, faith in the One who can calm the storms of nature and the storms of faith.

I have been pondering, meditating on peace …. A word, an idea, that is most often used at Christmas, maybe through the turning of a new year, spoken to or over us during times of tragedy, trauma; printed on clothing that represents the ideology of a generation. In each of these situations or seasons, peace means something completely different.

Even in the Word of God, there is a paradox of peace. Yet, though the contradiction is present, there is Truth in the contradiction.

> *"Peace I leave with you, My peace I give to you; not as the world gives do I give to you. Let not your heart be troubled, neither let it be afraid."* (John 14:27 NKJV)

In Isaiah 9:6, Isaiah prophetically calls the not-yet-come Jesus, Prince of Peace. Peace in this passage is the Hebrew word Shalom, meaning health, security, tranquility; a satisfied condition, an unconcerned state of peacefulness. This "peace" is a state of being.

However, to the contrary, Jesus, as recorded in Matthew 10:34 and Luke 12:51, tells His disciples, tells us today, "Do not think that I came to bring peace on earth. I did not come to bring peace but a sword." He is saying, "I did not come to bring rest from strife. I did not come to end striving and fighting, here and now." Peace, in these verses, in most places throughout the New Testament, means rest; in contrast with strife; denoting the absence or end of strife.

Reading the Epistles, peace is spoken as a greeting, a blessing, to say, "Be at rest, my friend." Jesus, in these 2 verses, clearly says that He did not come to bring an end to striving and fighting, but to bring a sword. The Prince of Peace (Is.9:6) did not come to bring peace to the world. What??

*"Peace I leave with you, My peace I give to you; not as the
world gives do I give to you. Let not your heart be troubled,
neither let it be afraid."*

In Mark 4, we see the well-known, oft-told account of Jesus
speaking to the storm, the waves, "Peace, be still!" Jesus and the
disciples have been walking for days. Jesus has healed all the sick
and taught the multitudes. Now, He wants to cross the lake; the same
lake where He found and called Peter, Andrew, James and John to
come follow Him. It's their lake…the one where they learned to
fish and sail. Jesus lays down to sleep while the guys do the work
of getting to the other side.

Then the unexpected…a storm that is big enough that these men,
the men who grew up on this lake, were afraid. They woke Jesus,
"Don't you care that we are dying?!" Jesus speaks to the wind and
waves, "Peace, be still." The wind and waves stop….immediately.
Peace, here, means an involuntary silence, stillness. Involuntary!
He commands nature to change course, to stop what it is doing.

I think He was also speaking to the hearts of the men with Him….
Peace, be still. Why do I think that? Because He then asks the
men, "Why are you so fearful? How is it that you have no faith?"

*"Peace I leave with you, My peace I give to you; not as the
world gives do I give to you. Let not your heart be troubled,
neither let it be afraid."*

If we continue reading in John 16:33, Jesus says, "…in Me, you
will have peace, but in the world you will have tribulation." How
can that be that we live, simultaneously in tribulation and peace?
Tribulation and rest, an absence of strife….???

Paul writes to the Romans, telling them that "..having been

justified by faith, we have peace through our Lord Jesus Christ."
We have REST, an absence of strife, by our faith through Jesus,
the Christ.

"Peace I leave with you, My peace I give to you; not as the
world gives do I give to you. Let not your heart be troubled,
neither let it be afraid."

The peace of God is not about our external circumstances or
realities. The Earth is groaning and travailing with natural disasters,
war, persecutions, genocides, and sickness. There is much to be
concerned about. There is much to pray over. My heart has a hole
in it. Some days…most days…that hole feels like a gigantic black
hole, sucking every other part of me in. Yet, if I simply change my
focus and settle my heart, there is a crazy, ridiculous, contradictory
peace at work in me. I strive against it some days. Some days, I just
want to be angry; I want to demand answers and understanding;
I want my version of justice, and I want to negotiate with God for
my obedience.

Peter was walking on water! Then the sight of the waves distracted
him again and he began to sink. His situation didn't change. Jesus
didn't take the time to explain what was happening. Peter looked
away and began to sink.

Peace is about perspective and perseverance. My friend, peace
and grace be unto you! May the Prince of Peace, Immanuel, be
so present in your heart that ***Truth would conquer your reality***.
Reality changes from moment to moment. Truth is Truth always,
and He has given you His peace that you, that I, would be at rest
in the tribulations of life.

PEACE IN THE STORM

Michelle so succinctly puts into words what we've been getting to throughout this book. Disappointment and peace can coexist. Grief and peace can coexist. Most often, the "peace" we're looking for is in the absence of tribulation and suffering. The peace Jesus offers us, most often, is found in the midst of that very storm. That's why He tells His disciples, "...not as the world gives...."

Peace is not a thing or a solution, it is a person, and His name is Jesus. He does not change. When we are in His presence, we are in the presence of peace. That's why it is vital we develop a culture in our lives, in our family, and in our other communities of pursuing the presence of God. In His presence there is peace, even in the raging storms.

Did you know?

Fear has no authority over you; only the authority you give it. But, if we keep our eyes on the Prince of Peace, we can walk on water, even while the storms are still raging. There will be times in our lives when Jesus calms our storms and gives us rest from them, but there will also be times when the storms will be hurricane level 5 and He will offer us His peace in the midst of it while He takes us to the other side. It's in those times we will walk on the water if we don't take our eyes of the One who makes it possible.

> *"God cannot give us a happiness and peace apart from Himself, because it is not there. There is no such thing."*
>
> **~ C. S. Lewis**

Prayer

Dear Heavenly Father,

Thank you for your peace, your Son, your sacrifice. I want to be able to sleep on the boat in the midst of the storm just like you did. I also want you to teach me how to step out of the boat, even when the waves are crashing and the storm is raging, and walk on water. Remind me of my mandate to walk in your authority and take dominion; to walk in your power and to not give into fear. The enemy will not kill, steal, or destroy my purpose. I choose you. I love you.

In the mighty name of Jesus I pray, amen.

19

THIS IS NOT OUR HOME

"My home is in heaven. I'm just passing through this world."

~ Billy Graham

(American evangelist)

DISTRACTIONS

For most of my life I've known about Jesus. I gave my heart to Him at the age of eight and was baptized. I still remember that day. My young heart, as ignorant and naive as it was, was truly after His heart. However, in my mind, heaven has always been something great that happens after you live a long and wonderful life.

I remember at the age of fifteen saying, "I want Jesus to return, but not until after I'm married." After I married Michelle, I remember thinking, "I want Jesus to return soon, but not until after I have children." After that it became seeing my children get married and then holding my grandchildren...and the list goes on and on.

My point is that there is never a "convenient" time to die. There are always more things to see and do. Consequently, if we allow them, they will distract us from our upward call. We lose sight of the stated fact this world is not our home. We are transient aliens here, migrant workers. We have a purpose and a mandate, but it's temporary.

I believe this is where disappointment is meant to play its part, if we allow it. We've already established our heavenly Father does not have evil planned for our lives. He has created us for greatness.

> *"For I know the thoughts that I think toward you, says the Lord, thoughts of peace and not of evil, to give you a future and a hope."* (Jeremiah 29:11 NKJV)

However, He will take those things that were intended to do us harm and take us out, and He will turn them around for our good. Genesis 50:20 (paraphrase)

LONGING FOR HOME

We need to be disappointed with this world, not infatuated with it. It can be alluring and enticing, but it is actually full of pain and suffering. Our disappointment, coupled with the Holy Spirit's revelation and grace, will drive us to long for our true home. It will keep us from losing sight of who we truly are, kingdom ambassadors, and help us to stay focused on the fact this life and all of its problems are temporal.

Before our daughter passed away, I would have told you I longed for Jesus' return, but it would not have been the truth. I was looking more to my future on this planet than I was to eternity with my Savior. I was thinking about my retirement and financial security. I was looking to the longevity of the ministry and the legacy I would leave behind. I was thinking about those grandbabies and what they would grow up to become. I was looking to live out the remainder of my life with Michelle in comfort, peace, and purpose. I'm guessing our plans were not much different from anyone else's when it comes to thinking about the future.

Yet, as I sat considering what we had lost in the days following our daughter's homegoing, I found none of those things had a hold on me any longer. I am longing for my home. I am longing for the comforting arms of my Heavenly Father.

Don't get me wrong, I will thoroughly enjoy walking my youngest daughter down the aisle when she finds that young man God has placed in front of her, and I will be "over the moon" with joy when I hold that first grandbaby and any others who follow. Michelle and I will continue to enjoy all the ministry, travels, and life God puts before us, but none of that will ever have a "hold" on me again. Every day I will pray for Him to come, and I will look to the heavens with hopeful expectation today might be that day.

I long for those "walks in the garden in the cool of the day." I am near tears when I think of my Savior revealing the mysteries of His creation to me as I sit at His feet.

I love how C.S. Lewis describes it in the last chapter of his last book in the *Chronicles of Narnia*:

"And as He spoke He no longer looked to them like a lion; but the things that began to happen after that were so great and beautiful that I cannot write them. And for us this is the end of all the stories, and we can most truly say that they all lived happily ever after. But for them it was only the beginning of the real story. All their life in this world and all their adventures in Narnia had only been the cover and the title page: now at last they were beginning Chapter One of the Great Story which no one on earth has read: which goes on forever: in which every chapter is better than the one before."[21]

While the *Chronicles of Narnia* is a work of fiction, C.S. Lewis' words, I believe, were meant to mirror another work that is NOT fiction, but the truth of our future written by John the Beloved but revealed by our heavenly Father,

"And I heard a loud voice from the throne saying, 'Behold, the dwelling place of God is with man. He will dwell with them, and they will be his people, and God himself will be with them as their God. He will wipe away every tear from their eyes, and death shall be no more, neither shall there be mourning, nor crying, nor pain anymore, for the former things have passed away.'

And he who was seated on the throne said, 'Behold, I am making all things new.'" (Revelation 21:3-4 ESV)

My heart yearns for the other side of eternity. It's my home and I cannot wait to be there. My disappointment and grief brought me to this place of hope. They could have delivered me to a darker place, a place devoid of light, joy, and peace, but instead of becoming lost in the darkness, I decided, I led and governed myself, to turn toward the light. I allowed my Savior to put me on a new path. I stopped resisting and I surrendered to His will and to His presence.

Our journey is not done. Remember C.S. Lewis said, this has "only been the cover and the title page." Michelle and I are still a work in progress. Our marriage is not perfect because we are not perfect. Our children are not perfect, and our lives are far from it. We are living from valley to valley and from glory to glory. This is not our home, and it never will be. Every chapter will be better than the one before. Our story this side of eternity is still being written.

FINAL THOUGHTS

Faster Daddy, Faster

It was around midnight when my wife began to have hard contractions. Nothing unusual about that with a pregnancy…it was the sudden exclamation, "I feel like I want to push," that threw everything into panic mode.

We were thirty-five minutes from the hospital. I had timed it several times the previous month. We had received a newsletter from friends who had just had a baby in their car because they didn't make it to the hospital in time. I was determined to NOT let that happen to us.

But here we were thirty-five minutes from the hospital and Michelle said she wanted to push. We grabbed the "go" bag, threw everything in the car and started out of the driveway. Michelle told me again, in case I had forgotten, "Mark, I feel like I need to push."

"Don't push!" I told her.

She gritted her teeth and said, "You just drive, I'm not going to push!"

Fortunately, there was very little traffic at midnight, and I drove a very unrighteous speed all the way. What was timed at thirty-five minutes, I was able to accomplish in nineteen!

Thirty minutes after pulling up to the emergency exit, I held Alyssa Ruth Moore in my arms. She entered the world the same way she lived and exited it…FULL SPEED AHEAD.

With Aly, there were always ONLY two speeds. Full stop or full speed. She had no speed control and no neutral. Just PARK and GO.

Unfortunately for her mother and me, when we wanted her to be full speed, she was usually full stop. And, when we wanted her to be full stop, she was full speed ahead. Aly was a handful. She was hard-headed and very stubborn. No matter what we did to correct her, she was determined to have her way. She would weigh the cost of her actions and then jump in with both feet, fully committed.

To give you an example of what we dealt with, when she was barely eighteen months old, we went to a friend's house to swim. We all sat at a table beside the pool when we heard a splash. We looked up, and Aly was at the bottom of the pool. We jumped in, grabbed her, and pulled her out. She coughed a few times and started laughing. Michelle dried her off and set her down next to the table. We gave her a stern and very worried warning never to do that again. Whew. Disaster avoided. Everyone's hearts raced.

No sooner had we begun to calm down than we looked up just as Aly ran toward the pool again. Splash. Straight to the bottom. She had counted the cost and decided the fun outweighed the trouble she would get into and the potential danger. We pulled her out a second time, coughing and laughing. Full speed ahead.

This was Aly. No matter how much we tried to "control" her life and discipline her poor behavior, it was like catching the wind. She would not be tamed. But Michelle and I wouldn't change it for anything…it's who she was. It's who she was created to be. It's the way she lived her life.

When she fully gave her heart to the Lord at seventeen, it was the same way. It was at full speed. She pursued Him with everything in her. He became her focus, her pursuit. She struggled just like every other teenager and twenty year old. She wanted to be married, she wanted to be liked, and she wanted to be loved. She was sassy and obstinate, hardheaded and stubborn. There were times where she was willfully disobedient, and no matter what we did to discipline her, it had ZERO effect. She made a lot of poor choices and had to live with a lot of tough consequences, which many times she found hurt worse than the discipline would have. Through it all, she grew and matured, and she allowed the Holy Spirit to mold and shape her.

In the end, she was following hard after Jesus. She was full speed ahead in her pursuit. That same hardheaded, stubborn approach to childhood became a determined focus to know her Heavenly Father. Michelle and I have had the honor of reading some of her journal writings...something we would NEVER have been allowed to do if she were still with us. We have been utterly amazed at her vulnerability and honest desire to experience a deep, tangible relationship with Jesus Christ even in the midst of her failures.

I've copied one of those writings from one of her last posts on Instagram (exactly as she wrote it). I hope this will challenge you as much as it has challenged us. She wrote this right after her twentieth birthday, three weeks before she slipped into eternity:

"i was created to love like a child. i can be so impulsive and i just want to love people in the moment with whatever i have on hand. i can be so so loud, very loud...and sometimes overwhelming for people around me. my teenage years are closed and i have really been struggling with it. thinking i need to be someone completely different when i turn twenty. that i need to be super calm and collected. that i need to be mature and use big words and all that. honestly, i still miss my mom, i hate doing my own laundry, and i wish i didn't have to cook my own meals. i forgot that i was created to be aly and that that's enough (even if i'm twenty now). i don't usually make long posts like this but i wanted to encourage you guys, you're enough the way you are. i'm always in the hunt for adventure, i get in trouble a lot for it, and i usually make a mess during the process. i apologize often and i laugh through everything. that's okay, because that's who i am."

When you lose a child at a young age, it's hard to see anything good in it, but then I began to see all the lives my little girl touched in her short twenty years. I began to see the true nature of her relationship with the One whom Michelle and I have given our lives to pursue—Jesus Christ. She took the baton and ran full speed ahead. I realized at that moment, she still has a message to relay to everyone, and this is how I want to close our time together.

Her simple but powerful message is this: "Don't stop and don't delay. Get in the race. It's not too late to start running, you just have to change your speed."

Some of you have been at full-stop, some at half speed. Maybe it's because of your own loss and pain. You can't quite seem to find your pace any longer. Aly's cry to all of us today is, "It's ALL OR NOTHING!" There is NO neutral. There is no speed control. It's FULL SPEED ahead!

As my Aly girl would say, "Faster, Daddy. Faster!"

CONCLUSION

It's hard to believe this is the end of the book. I feel I have so much more to say, while also feeling I've said enough. Perhaps there will be a part 2; a "rest of the story" as the popular radio broadcaster, Paul Harvey said. I know we still have a lot of the story left to live, a lot left to learn. That's what a journey is all about.

There will be amazing sites to see, fun things to do, and great accomplishments to achieve. There will also be engine trouble, flat tires, and wrecks along the way. That's life. The question is: Will the unplanned difficulties of the journey crush the beautiful times or will they lead us to a better understanding of our creator and make us more like Him?

This is the crossroads where we often find ourselves. What direction will we go? The choice will always be ours. Nothing in this book matters if we don't choose Him, if we don't choose worship; it all hinges on that.

Choices. Every day. All day.

They will define your future, and they will define your walk with the Lord. That's important because He is the only One who can bring peace. He is the only One who can bring joy. Everything else is just a Band-Aid, a quick fix on a lifelong problem.

He is your hope, and He is the answer to your disappointment, pain, and grief. It's time you start walking on water. So, get out of the boat.

In Him, through Him and FOR Him,
Mark

NOTES

1. Tozer, A.W. *The Crucified Life*. Bloomington: Bethany House Publisher, 2011.

2. Keller, Timothy. 2014. *@timkellernyc: Twitter*. December 6. https://mobile.twitter.com/timkellernyc/status/541331745313148928?lang=id.

3. Johnson, Bill. *God is Good: He's Better Than You Think*. Shippensburg: Destiny Image, 2016.

4. Munroe, Myles. *Overcoming Crisis*. Destiny Image, 2009.

5. TerKeurst, Lysa. *It's Not Supposed to Be This Way*. Nashville: Thomas Nelson, 2018.

6. Maureen Sharphouse website, *"Live a Life of No Limits,"* accessed September 15, 2021, https://www.maureensharphouse.com/2019/08/07/a-life-of-constant-bliss-would-teach-us-nothing-we-need-both-the-highest-highs-and-the-lowest-lows/.

7. Spurgeon, Charles. *Letters to My Students*. Grand Rapids: Zondervan, 1954.

8. Michelle Ule website, *"Thank you Elisabeth Elliot,"* accessed September 15, 2021, https://www.michelleule.com/2015/06/15/thank-you-elisabeth-elliot/.

9. Goff, Bob. 2016. *@bobgoff: Twitter*. December 16. https://twitter.com/bobgoff/status/942032282570833920?lang=en.

10. Ortberg, John. *Eternity is Now in Session*. Carol Stream: Tyndale House Publishers, Inc., 2018.

11. Elliot, Elisabeth. *Shadow of the Almighty*. New York: HarperCollins, 2009.

12. Batterson, Mark. *Going All In*. Grand Rapids: Zondervan, 2013.

13. Lewis, C.S. *Reflections on the Psalms*. New York: Harcourt, Brace & Co., 1958.

14. Billington, Ray. *Religion Without God*. New York: Routledge, 2002.

15. Tozer, A.W. *The Pursuit of God*. Mansfield Centre: Martino Publishing, 1948.

16. Ibid

17. Ibid

18. Ann Voskamp website, *"When you need to know it's okay not to be okay,"* accessed September 15, 2021, https://annvoskamp.com/2018/10/when-you-need-to-know-its-okay-not-to-be-okay/.

19. Sheila Walsh website, *"I will rise,"* https://sheilawalsh.com/i-will-rise/.

20. Kalemati website, accessed September 15, 2021, https://kalemati.net/topic/Glimpse?page=6.

21. Lewis, C.S. *The Last Battle*. New York, New York: HarperCollins, 1956.

Made in the USA
Monee, IL
29 July 2022

10481936R00098